SPOKEN
from HEART
the

SELWYN HUGHES

SPOKEN
from
the HEART

POWERFUL TALKS AND ADDRESSES THAT HAVE BLESSED
AND INSPIRED AUDIENCES AROUND THE WORLD BY

SELWYN HUGHES

Published 2005 by CWR, Waverley Abbey House, Waverley Lane, Farnham, Surrey GU9 8EP, England.

See back of book for list of National Distributors.

Unless otherwise indicated, all Scripture references are from the Holy Bible: New International Version (NIV), copyright © 1973, 1978, 1984 by the International Bible Society.
Other versions indicated:
AV: The Authorised Version
NKJV: New King James Version, © 1982, Thomas Nelson Inc.

Front cover image: Jeffery Howe, Roger Walker
Concept development, editing, design and production by CWR

Printed in Finland by WS Bookwell

ISBN: 1-85345-376-5

~ CONTENTS ~

~ INTRODUCTION ~

For many years of my life I have been a travelling preacher. Nothing thrills me more than to stand in a pulpit or in front of a lectern in a local church and 'preach the Word'. I can think of no greater privilege and honour in all the world than to be a 'spokesman for God' when His people gather together for prayer and worship.

I have always been glad that God called me to be a preacher. I am told that when I was an infant and my parents dedicated me to God (the Nonconformist version of 'infant baptism') the pastor who took me in his arms and prayed over me paused at the end of his prayer and added as a kind of postscript: 'And Lord I ask that You will make this child into a preacher of the gospel.'

Once, when talking to a group of Christian leaders and invited representatives (school teachers, lawyers, doctors, counsellors and so on) in Chennai, India, I told that story and said, 'I would rather be a preacher than the King of England.'

A young man who was present was so affected by that remark that he could not get it out of his mind for days. He consulted his pastor and after prayer together they felt this was the Lord's way of impressing upon him that he was being called to the ministry. He entered Bible college and today is one of India's great preachers.

The sermons or talks contained in this first volume (of what may become a series) have been preached in many different parts of the world, the same sermon being preached sometimes more than once. I do not belong to that school of thought that believes a sermon should be only preached once and then scrapped. I am of the opinion that if a sermon is not worth preaching twice it is not worth preaching once.

I must have preached thousands of sermons in 55 years of ministry. I have notes of most of them. How did I decide which ones I would put in print? Largely my decision was influenced by people who have said to me over the years, 'I remember you preaching on ... it was a message that changed my life'. It has been said that a sermon should not be remembered but translated into life; however, it is very gratifying to a preacher that at least his sermons have been remembered!

A sermon or a talk given from the pulpit of a church is quite different from an essay. In my opinion an essay is quite out of place in the pulpit. Dr W.E. Sangster, the man who more than anyone else helped to shape my preaching ability, used to say, 'A sermon can combine exposition, rebuke, challenge, comfort ... it calls for direct speech. A preacher can say "You". Indeed he ought to say "You". He can almost point – if he points to himself as well!'

A sermon or a 'talk' must of necessity have shape. Even untutored minds appreciate form and the movement and progression and style. People know when a message begins crisply, takes shape as it moves forward and heads for a clear conclusion. Some of the 'sermons' and 'talks' I have heard in church remind me of the text in Genesis 1:1: 'The earth was without form, and void; and darkness was on the face of the deep' (NKJV).

I am coming to the stage in my life when my preaching engagements are getting fewer and fewer, not because of the lack of invitations but because illness prevents me from travelling as much as I used to. That is why I send forth this first book of my talks and sermons with a prayer that, as they have blessed those who heard me preach them, they will also bless those who read them.

Selwyn Hughes
Waverley Abbey House,
Farnham, Surrey.
2005

1

GLEANINGS
FROM THE
GLEAMINGS

1 KINGS 6:29–30

On the walls all around the temple, in both the inner and outer rooms, he carved cherubim, palm trees and open flowers. He also covered the floors of both the inner and outer rooms of the temple with gold.

This verse came alive for me some time ago in the middle of Kuala Lumpur airport, Malaysia. I had been in the country to speak at a businessmen's conference and on the final Sunday I was asked to preach in one of my most favourite churches in all the world – the Full Gospel Assembly in downtown KL. It is a most wonderful church with over 10,000 members, many of whom are *Every Day with Jesus* readers.

At the end of the day I was taken by some friends to the international airport to wait for the British Airways flight to London. After checking in and taking my seat in the departure lounge a message came through the public address system to say that the flight to London would be delayed by one hour.

Experience has taught me to be prepared for delays at airports and that is why I always carry with me a new book I am reading, or a notepad on which I can write notes or expand any new ideas that might be running through my mind. On this occasion however I decided to take out my Bible and read through the book of 1 Kings. I had committed myself in that year to reading through the whole Bible from Genesis to Revelation and the appropriate reading for the day was 1 Kings chapters 6 to 8.

I read the first 28 verses of chapter 6 and when I came to verse 29

– the verse I have taken as my text – a rather strange thing happened. The chapter deals with the building of Solomon's temple and the description of the inner temple which was lined with pure gold, and as I read, it seemed as if in my imagination I had entered a time tunnel and I pictured what it would be like to stand in a room whose walls were covered with gold.

I reflected particularly on the fact that on those gleaming gold walls Solomon had carved the figures of cherubim, palm trees and open flowers. What could those symbols mean? I asked myself.

Before I share with you the conclusions I came to that day let me say a few words about this amazing temple that Solomon built. What a magnificent construction it was. Altogether it took seven years to build. Every stone was cut and shaped some distance from the site so that no sound of a hammer was heard.

What intrigued me most was the fact that the inside of the temple was covered with pure gold. Almost everything within it also was covered with gold – the chains, the altar and the cherubim. But the thing that grabbed my attention there in the middle of Kuala Lumpur airport was the detail laid out in the 29th verse – the carved figures of cherubim, palm trees and open flowers.

THE CHERUBIM

I let my mind run over what I knew about cherubim in Scripture. Everywhere they are seen at worship. Their very existence spells out the fact they were created for that purpose. And that too I suggest is the *primary* reason for our existence. The very first reason for us being here on this earth is not to establish a career, form a family, write books (or even sell books), counsel, organise conferences or evangelise – it is to worship God. All the things I just mentioned are important but we must see that first and foremost God wants us to worship Him. Nothing can be more important than that.

I have been an evangelical for 60 years and a minister for 55 years. One of the things I have noticed in the years that I have been a firsthand observer of what goes on in the Christian Church is the ease with which believers can allow the things that ought to be first to become second in their lives.

Often when being interviewed I have been asked, 'What in your opinion is the biggest occupational hazard for those involved in Christian work and ministry?' My answer is always this: *It is becoming more interested in the cause of Christ than in Christ Himself.* It is possible to be taken up more with the things of the Lord than the Lord Himself.

The Bible college where I did my training had this as a motto: 'Let me never lose the important truth that I must love Thyself more than Thy service.' Now despite seeing that motto every day I have to hang my head in shame because when I came into the ministry I became more zealous for the work of the Lord than I did for the Lord Himself. It makes me sad to admit this but I was more interested in working for Him than worshipping Him.

Oh, I would worship Him of course, but my biggest desire was to get into the community and work in such a way that I could see the impact of my own efforts in souls coming to Christ and in people being helped. I liked the feeling that what I was doing had spiritual repercussions in the lives of people. Deep down I was more interested in getting something for myself rather than giving, which of course is what worship essentially is.

All this begs the question: Why does God want us to worship Him? When I was a young student this issue used to concern me a great deal.

I have to confess that in those early days I went around with the idea that perhaps God was egotistical, like some vain man or woman who continually sought for compliments.

It was C.S. Lewis who put me right on this. First, he said, worship is the right response to such a Creator as this. We are made by God, he pointed out, to appreciate the beautiful and recoil from the ugly. Just as admiring a magnificent painting or a beautiful scene is a right response, so is worship the right response to such a wonderful Creator. Those who delight in the ugly and are repelled by the beautiful are perverted.

Often when counselling Christians with psychological problems, I have said to them: 'What does the word "worship" mean to you?' They have replied in words similar to these: 'Not very much' or 'Not a great deal'. I have found that people who are psychologically troubled find it difficult to worship; they are bounded very much by their own ego. They focus more on themselves than on God. This is of course because they are in pain.

When you have a toothache you don't feel very much like going out and knocking at people's doors and trying to engage them in a conversation about Christian things. Pain has the tendency to focus you on yourself. I have often said to my students doing counsellor training that first and foremost Christian counselling is releasing people from preoccupation with themselves to preoccupation with the worship of God.

Lewis has a great line in connection with the things I have just been saying: 'Worship is inner health made audible.' True worshippers are healthy on the inside because their focus is not self-centred but God-centred. Those involved in helping us worship are caught up in one of the greatest ministries possible – not greater than the ministry of the Word of God perhaps, but in my opinion equal to it.

Another thing Lewis said about worship is that it is in going through the door of worship that we make it possible for God to come to us. As we give ourselves to Him He is then able to give Himself to us. It is not only for His sake that He encourages us to worship but also for ours. In the act of worshipping Him we open the door through which He can give Himself to us and draw our souls to inner health. We are the beneficiaries of worship, as well as God. As we worship Him our souls are drawn to health and we become all the better for worshipping.

Lewis also pointed out that although there is only a fine line between worship and praise there really is a difference. We praise God for what He does for us, we worship Him for who He is. He said, 'When I learned how a thing can be revered not for what it can do for me, but for what it is in itself, then I understood the difference between praise and worship.'

At this point in my musings I heard the public address system crackle into life and the announcer say: 'The British Airways flight to London is now ready for boarding.' As an experienced traveller I knew I had at least another half an hour to meditate on the carved figures on the golden gleaming walls of Solomon's temple, as it usually takes an hour to get people on board a jet. So I allowed myself to slip back into the time tunnel and ponder now the significance of the carved figure of the palm tree.

THE PALM TREE

I let my mind run over what I knew about the palm tree. I remembered reading somewhere that a palm tree has hundreds of different uses. Its fruit, its wood, its sap, its husk, its fibre, all can be used. Thus it is a symbol of usefulness and service.

The message, then, that comes from the palm tree is quite simply this: God wants us to be contributors to His kingdom. He has saved us not only that we might worship Him but also in order that we might serve Him. He wants us to be busily engaged in working for Him, in being His ambassadors to this godless generation.

But it is important when we consider that God wants us to be His workers that we remember we are to be worshippers first and workers second. That is the divine order. If we put work first and worship second then we get it wrong. Our work must flow out of worship.

In the years that I have been a follower of Jesus Christ I have come to see that the central fact of the Christian life is not what we can do for Him but what He has done for us. Let me explain what I mean by that. Often in a counselling session a person has said to me something like this: 'My problem is I don't love the Lord enough'. I have usually responded to that kind of statement by saying, 'No, that is not your problem; your problem is you don't know how much the Lord loves you'.

I would then go on to explain that the love we have for Christ is our response to His love for us. A text that I love so much ever since I came to understand its profound truth is this: 'We love because he first loved us' (1 John 4:19). Ask yourself the question: How did I become a Christian? Did you say to yourself one day, 'I am going to become a follower of the Lord Jesus Christ and I am going to set my heart in the direction of loving Him'? No, what happened was that the Spirit brought home to your heart the realisation that Christ had died for your sin on the cross and as you received that revelation, the scales fell from your eyes, and in response to His love for you, your love flamed back. Our love for Christ is a response to His love for us. As an old Welsh woman once put it to me: 'He did the courtin''.

That is why whenever people say to me that they feel their love for Christ waning I advise them to linger prayerfully before the cross and focus on what it meant for Christ to have given His life for them. There is a law of the soul that goes like this: *What we think about affects the way we feel, and how we feel affects the way we act.* Our feelings follow our thoughts like little ducks on a pond follow their mother. Rarely will a person come away from meditating on what Jesus did for them on the cross without their own love rising in response to the love that He demonstrated for them there.

Another thing I have noticed as I have mingled with the great Christians that have come across my path in the years that I have followed Christ is this: the best worshippers make the best workers. Paul the apostle is the great illustration of this. Take for example his great writings in the epistle to the Romans where he deals with such profound subjects as condemnation, justification, sanctification, consecration, and so on and then in the midst of the most taxing theology he suddenly bursts forth in impassioned praise.

> Oh, the depth of the riches of the wisdom and knowledge
>   of God!
>   How unsearchable his judgments,
>   and his paths beyond tracing out!
> 'Who has known the mind of the Lord?
>   Or who has been his counsellor?'
> 'Who has ever given to God,
>   that God should repay him?'
> For from him and through him and to him are all things.
>   To him be the glory forever! Amen.
>
> Rom. 11:33–36

Paul, you see, was a worshipping man and the work he did for God flowed out of his worshipping spirit. There is little doubt in my mind, based on my experience and my contact with multiplied thousands of Christians over the years, that the best worshippers make the best and most productive workers.

I was in Adelaide, Australia, some years ago, speaking at a conference, and I met there a retired missionary by the name of Tommy Evans. Tommy was a Welshman and I can remember when I was a little boy in Wales my father, who was the missionary secretary of the local church, always mentioning the name Tommy Evans, who at that time worked in India, and urging us to pray for him. So it was interesting for me to meet up with him and tell him how my father had faithfully prayed for him during the time of his missionary work in India. Tommy Evans was 90 years of age and legally blind when I met him and during the conference he was asked to speak for a few minutes to the delegates about his present circumstances and how he was spending his sunset years in the service of God.

He told us how during the previous week he had taken his grandson with him into the bush, miles from Adelaide, to witness to a small community there. Led from house to house by his grandson he talked to the people there about Christ and won a number of them to the Lord. Then he set up the foundations of a small church and arranged for someone to go and disciple them and help them in the nurture of their faith.

As I listened to this 90-year-old man tell this story I burst into tears. A minister sitting next to me on the platform said, 'Are you all right?' I explained as quietly as I could that my heart had been deeply moved as I realised that I was listening to a man who, though 90 years of age, was sold out in the service of Jesus Christ. I knew I was in the presence of a worshipping man who was also a great worker.

There was a woman in a church I once pastored who told me she used to like to come to the end of the week – empty. She let her petrol tank become almost empty, her purse, her fridge and so on. At first I thought she was a little strange and in need of counselling but she told me that her aim in doing this was to remind herself that when she leaves this world she should go having given away the blessings God had given her! 'I need to do this,' she said, 'to remind myself not to hoard what God has given to me spiritually.'

Some thought that woman to be a little eccentric but in fact she was one of the greatest soul-winners I have ever known. I asked her to explain her eccentricity to the rest of the congregation one day and she said, 'When I come to stand before the Lord I don't want Him to say: "Do you have anything left that I gave you? Did you give it all away?" ' That's what I think it means to carry the palm – to share with others what God has shared with us.

At this point in my meditation there came the sharp tones of the announcer on the public address system again: 'This is the last call for the flight to London.' I could see from where I sat there were about 60 or 70 people still in line and I knew I had at least another 15 minutes, so I slipped back into the time tunnel and let my imagination take over once again.

I had reflected on what the cherubim meant and the palm tree but what about the third item?

THE OPEN FLOWER

In my younger days flowers never meant much to me. I hardly saw them. My wife who loved them used to say to me, 'Look at those beautiful flowers', and I would say 'Where?' Then she would name them and tell me about them and eventually I came to love them in the same way she did.

What does the carved figure of the open flower in Solomon's temple suggest to us? It speaks of the sweet smell of the loveliness of the kingdom of heaven spread out on earth in the lives of God's children. The beauty of lives that know God.

In this dark and depressing world in which we live there is so much that is unlovely, so much that is grim and dour and dismal and depressing. There is much that is beautiful too of course but I am referring to the spiritual darkness that is all around us. God wants us as His people to brighten the spiritual drabness and the dismal conditions which sin has brought about by spreading like open flowers the sweet perfume of His loveliness all around. In this way we become witnesses to His amazing grace.

There comes to mind an occasion when I visited a friend on her birthday and I took with me a bunch of the most beautiful flowers I had purchased from a supermarket shelf. The flowers looked so lovely and exquisite that I remember thinking to myself: 'She will be thrilled with these wonderfully rich colours.' When I presented them to her she received them graciously and after a while when I noticed that she made no effort to put them in water, I said: 'Wouldn't it be a good idea to put the flowers in water now as it has been some time since I bought them?'

She looked at me with a smile and said, 'These flowers can live for a long time without water. Obviously you didn't realise that they are artificial!'

You can imagine my discomfiture at that moment and from that day to this you can be sure I have been extra careful when buying flowers for someone.

Now at this point in my imaginative exploration of Solomon's temple the PA system crackled into life again and the announcer said, 'Will the last remaining passenger for the BA flight to London go at once to the departure gate which is about to close.'

I reluctantly raced down the time tunnel back into the world of reality, picked up my briefcase realising it was now time to go. As I walked onto the plane my heart was singing an old chorus that sadly many in today's church do not seem to know:

> Let the beauty of Jesus be seen in me.
> All His wondrous compassion and purity
> O Thou Spirit divine
> All my nature refine,
> Till the beauty of Jesus be seen in me.

As it was past midnight when the plane took off I told the stewardess I didn't want anything to eat. I put on my eye shades provided by the airline and soon drifted into sleep with the thoughts I have just shared with you on my mind.

What then do the incarnations of the cherubim, the palm tree and the flowers carved on the walls of the house of God in both inner and outer rooms mean? Those who experience God in worship will find that it leads to service for Him, and the service we give to Him and for Him spreads like open flowers the perfume of His loveliness to all around.

We are called by the sacred symbolism of Scripture to be worshippers, workers and witnesses to His grace. And as we respond like the palm tree moved by the wind it is then that our lives will bring beauty where ugliness reigns and spread the perfume of the grace of Christ in this dark damp dungeon we call a world.

So I remind you again that we are called to be nothing less than worshippers, workers and witnesses to His grace.

That is what I gleaned in the middle of Kuala Lumpur airport from the Temple's Golden Gleaming Walls.

2

'BECAUSE ...'

DEUTERONOMY 7:7–9

The Lord did not set **his affection** on you and choose you because you were more numerous than other peoples, for you were the fewest of all peoples. But it was *because* the Lord loved you and kept the oath he swore to your forefathers that he brought you out with a mighty hand and redeemed you from the land of slavery, from the power of Pharaoh king of Egypt. (My emphasis.)

Several years ago, whilst talking to a group of church elders and deacons prior to my taking the pulpit in their church, they told me the following story. Some months previously they had been in need of an interregnum minister to lead their congregation and so they invited a few Bible students who were about to graduate to preach a trial sermon in their church. One of the students, they told me, preached a fascinating and intriguing sermon from the text: 'But Naaman was a leper' (2 Kings 5:1, AV).

Apparently the young student's whole thesis was built around the world 'but'. He expostulated on the thought that without that little conjunction the English language would be so much poorer. He spent 30 minutes giving examples of how some sentences would just not make sense unless the word 'but' was included.

Later, when the deacons and church elders met with the young man to discuss his trial sermon, one of the leading elders said: 'Young man, you have preached a singularly impressive sermon and given us a great deal of food for thought, especially in the area of grammar. I myself have been educated on how a little thing like a conjunction can play such an important part in communication' ... and then with a twinkle in his eye he added, 'But you are not the man for the pulpit of this church, that is very clear.'

Now, at the risk of repeating that unfortunate youth's mistake, I myself want to take one word as a text: it is not 'but'; it is 'because'. Listen again to what Moses says to God's ancient people, the Israelites: 'The LORD did not set his affection on you and choose you because you were more numerous than other peoples, for you were the fewest of all peoples. But it was because the LORD loved you ...'

That word 'because', when used in a certain way, has been described by someone as 'the strangest, oldest, shortest and most intriguing response in the English language'. Those of you who are parents know from experience how after you have responded a dozen times to the same question from your children such as, 'Why can't I have another biscuit?' 'Why can't I wear my new shoes in bed?' 'Why do I have to go to school?' and having given every reasonable explanation you can think of yet your child persists in asking the same question over and over again, you fall back on that strangest, oldest, shortest and most intriguing response in the English language – 'Because'.

I am sure that, like me, there have been many times in your life when you have been in a situation where you wished you had the sharpness to come up with a smart and clever answer to a question that would silence your questioner, whether it be your child or someone else. Like the grocer's assistant I heard about who was asked by a woman for half a lettuce. He walked into the back of the shop and said to the manager, 'There's a stupid woman outside who has asked for half a lettuce' and then looking behind him and seeing that the woman had followed him into the back of the shop said, quick as a flash, 'And this nice lady would like the other half.'

It has been an interest of mine when travelling to other countries where English is not the first language, to ask parents how they handle their children when they respond with 'Why?' to every answer they are given. I have asked that question to ascertain if in other languages they adopt a similar response to the English word – because. I have been surprised that in almost every culture I have raised this matter, I have been informed that parents use a similar word to our 'because', and when faced with persistent questions from their children use it in precisely the same way we do.

Moses is saying something like this in the passage before us now. He is making the point that if the Israelites were looking for logical reasons as to why they had been delivered from Egypt's bondage and were on their way to the promised land, there were none – other than the fact that God loved them. 'It is not because you are more in number than the other nations,' he emphasises, 'it is simply because God loves you.'

Our human pride would like to be able to come up with clear and logical reasons why God should love us, such as our likeability, our attractive personalities, our resourcefulness, our engaging disposition ... and so on. A woman once said to me, 'I can't think of one reason why God should love me.' I replied, 'My dear, there is no reason. He loves because He can't help loving. Nothing in you gave rise to it and nothing in you can extinguish it.'

No theologian, no matter how educated or reputable, can adequately explain why God loves us. I have been trying to explain it for decades. I have now given up trying to explain it but I have not given up talking about it. I tell you, the greatest joy of my life is to stand and preach about it. I can think of no subject more wonderful and no topic more thrilling.

You see, to 'explain' the love of God would require that He loves us for something outside Himself, whilst the truth is He loves us for ourselves alone. That love has its fount in the depth of His own Being. He chooses to love us – just because He is love.

The great hymn writer Charles Wesley begins one of his hymns with these words: *'He hath loved, He hath loved us'* and I often wonder to myself what might have been in his mind as he pondered the next line. Would he try to give some reason for the divine love? No, he was too wise to try and come up with a reason as he knew full well there is no reason. So he wrote:

> He hath loved, He hath loved us,
> Because – He *would love.*

He chose to – just because He is love. He is such a God. As another hymnist has put it:

> It is love to the loveless shown
> Without reason and without end.

'One of the disadvantages of growing up in a Christian home,' said the late Dr W.E. Sangster, 'is that one always hears talk about the love of God and one becomes used to the phrase, we take it as part of the order of things. It is no more exciting than sunshine and air, though all the time we are living in it and are utterly dependent upon it, we take it for granted and seldom with gratitude. There is no wonder in it and no realisation in it either. God is remote and love is but a word.'

Although we cannot 'explain' the love of God perhaps it might help us if we thought for a moment how different it is from human love and also how much higher. Human love, for example, is *conditional*; divine love is *unconditional*. There are no strings to God's love. He does not love us if we will do this or that. He loves us for ourselves alone. It is love without condition and it is love without end.

In the face of this amazing love does not the poverty of our own love sweep over us? Human love is so often a bargaining kind of love: *I will love you if you will love me*. The love we give to others is more conditional than we often realise, though the condition is not always expressed. Underlying many of our so-called loving actions is the attitude: if you do this for me then you can count on my affection. Or, give me the kind of love I want, and my love will revive again. So much human love is love for something even when it masquerades as the love of God.

None of this is like the divine love. The unconditional love of God means that because we are not loved *for* anything no failure on our part can rob us of that love. We cannot even sin God's love away. We can never escape this inexorable and aggressive Lover. Blessed be His holy Name.

As the apostle Paul so wonderfully puts it in Romans, chapter 8 and verses 37–39:

> For I am convinced that neither death nor life, neither angels nor demons, neither the present nor the future, nor any powers, neither height nor depth, nor anything else in all creation, will be able to separate us from the love of God that is in Christ Jesus our Lord.

Consider this also – human love can be *tainted*; divine love is *untainted*. It has been said that the nearest to heaven of all the loves of earth is the love of a mother for her child. But not even that kind of love is exempt from being tainted. The intrusions of self are so thrustful and subtle that mother-love can quickly turn into 'smother' love where freedom to be oneself is denied to the child because of the mother's possessiveness. How resentful of other loves some mothers can be – even the love of a son for his sweetheart! How prodigal a mother's love can be in giving yet how fierce in retaining. It is sad that the best can be so easily perverted into the worst.

God's love however is not like that; it remains untainted in all situations and all circumstances. One writer says that one way we can tell the difference between human love and divine love is by asking two simple questions:

- Is it seeking to gain anything from the relationship or is it just love?
- Does it leave the recipient free?

The wonder of God's love is that it does not seek to gain anything from the relationship but delights to give whether it receives anything back or not. Perhaps this is what another writer was thinking of when he said, 'Love does not begin until it expects nothing in return'. Divine love also leaves men and women free to accept it or reject it and continues in its loving even though it is trampled underfoot.

Then again human love is *limited*; divine love *unlimited*. The great writer and poet William Shakespeare once wrote: 'Love is not love which alters when it alteration finds'. By that definition much of what we describe as human love is not really love at all. How often has a man or woman stood before a minister or a priest and made marriage vows that commit them to continue loving their spouse no matter what adverse circumstances might occur (for richer, for poorer, in sickness or in health and so on) only to find that after a while they run out of love? Human love can be fickle, changeable and ambivalent. Divine love – never.

I am reminded of the story of the young man who said to his

sweetheart as he was leaving her one evening, 'I would go through fire and water for you.' Then as he said goodnight he remarked, 'I'll see you tomorrow night if it is not raining!'

On the other hand of course there are many stories of human love going to great lengths of self-sacrifice in the interest of the one loved; but for every such story there are a dozen or more that show human love to be erratic, changeable and undependable.

Human love, generally speaking, has its limits.

The apostle Paul when writing to the Christians in Ephesus, emphasises the limitless love of God and prays that all believers 'may have power, together with all the saints, to grasp how wide and long and high and deep is the love of Christ, and to know this love that surpasses knowledge ...' (Eph. 3:18–19). Note the phrase '*together with all the saints*'.

It is as if the apostle is saying: 'It would be impossible for one Christian to comprehend the limitless love of God' but perhaps all of us together, with our differing perceptions and our individual evaluations acting corporately might get a little closer to understanding it. Closer perhaps, but we will never be able to fully comprehend it. The limitless love of God has been described as 'an ocean without a shore'. Its height and depth and length and breadth is beyond our ability to measure or compute.

An African poet, reflecting on the unlimited love of God, wrote these poignant and moving lines:

There's a limit to the number
  of the wondrous stars that shine,
There's a limit to the wealth of gold
  that's deep in every mine,
There's a limit to the number of

the blades of grass God made,
There's a limit to the number of
   the trees in every glade,
But I know when I gaze upon Calvary –
   that there isn't any limit to His love for me.

It has been said, 'God only knows the love of God – and only God can reveal it.' Well, as the lines we looked at a moment ago tell us, God has revealed it – the most burning expression of it – at the place called Calvary. The apostle John tells us that the only way we can love with the love that God has is when He reveals it to us and we allow it to penetrate deep into our hearts – 'We love because he first loved us' (1 John 4:19).

His agape produces agape in us. Heaven knows no higher strategy for begetting love in human hearts than by bringing us to the cross where, seeing how much we are loved, the scales fall from our eyes and our own love flames in response. Just seeing that love and having its meaning conveyed to us supernaturally by the Holy Spirit is enough. Our heart plays truant and runs to its rightful Lord.

One of the great mysteries of life is the mystery of love creating its own response. We open our hearts to the love of God as seen in Christ on the cross and we find that same love burning in our own hearts. It is by the revelation of His love to us that we can rise to an adoring love of Him. In the rapture of this love we love others. And when people ask us for an explanation of why we love we are as much at a loss to explain that as we are the love of God. 'Agape love,' said Dr Cynddylan Jones, a famous Welsh preacher, 'cannot be explained, it can only be enjoyed.'

Blaise Pascal, the famous French philosopher and mathematician (and also a Christian), said, 'The heart has reasons the head knows nothing of.' He pointed out something we are all aware of, that we so often determine preferences and make decisions, not on the basis of what is going on in our heads but in our hearts. We arrive at some of the greatest decisions of our lives based not so much on reason or logic but what is going on deep within us – in our hearts – and then we look for logical reasons to support our feelings.

Now this should not surprise us because we are made in God's image. We find within us a glorious illogicality, a strange unreasonableness that cannot be pinned down to logical explanations and definitions. You see, what I am talking about here is higher than reason. Why do I believe in eternity? Is it because my head says it? Is it because I have approached it from a logical point of view and thought it carefully through and through? Well that may well happen but I suspect a more true explanation is because God has put eternity in our hearts.

One of the things that has intrigued me as I have met up with fellow believers over the years who have done a great work for God, is to see how, when pressed to give reasons for the love that has prompted them to give their lives in self-sacrificing service for the cause of Christ, fall back on the pattern of their heavenly Father and simply say 'because'.

I have a friend in India who gave up a large church in the USA and the offer of a high position in the denomination he served, to move into an unsanitary village in the state of Kerala, South India, and minister to a small congregation of people numbering no more than 100.

He had been doing that for 20 years when I met him at a conference in Madras (now called Chennai) where I was speaking. I was curious as to why he would give up a situation where his influence could have been brought to bear upon thousands rather than just hundreds. I tried every way I could to get him to explain it to me. After I had probed and prodded and asked dozens of different questions to try and get him to come up with some logical reasons for his decision, he turned to me and with a smile, shrugged his shoulders and said, 'Because.' He was making the point that there wasn't really a logical explanation; it was something he felt prompted to do deep down in his heart.

It is the same with others of God's servants too. Wherever you find people spending themselves in service for others, with no great fame, no earthly rewards; a minister working in a small church perhaps, a faithful woman standing at the side of the man she loves, a businessman or woman who gives up a lucrative career to work in unprepossessing circumstances, and you press them for reasons as to why they continue loving in this way – what do they say? They say what Livingstone said in Africa, what Hudson Taylor said in China, what Jackie Pullinger said in Hong Kong, what Mother Teresa said in Calcutta ... The only reason I can give is a love flows in my heart begotten of the Holy Spirit. If you want a logical reason then I cannot give you one. It's just – because.

You see the Christian story is a love story and love stories are not arguable. The older I get in the Christian faith the more I realise that my faith does not rest on theological arguments. There was a time when it did. I knew all the arguments for the existence of God (the argument from Design, for example) and all the other arguments as to why God allowed sin to intrude into His universe, why He allows suffering and so on but nowadays my faith rests not so much on them but on the experiential knowledge that I am loved by the world's greatest Lover.

I know of nothing more wonderful in all of the experiences I have gone through in my life than sensing and feeling the divine love wrapping itself around my heart holding me safe and secure.

A few years ago I spoke at a conference in Zimbabwe organised by the British Evangelical Alliance. The highlight of the conference was a Saturday morning breakfast meeting when people gathered from many distant parts of the country, some travelling days to be there. Amongst them were many *Every Day with Jesus* readers who had read my words for years but had never met me personally.

The atmosphere was full of excitement and anticipation as I walked around the breakfast table meeting so many of my readers. Following breakfast I spoke to them on the theme of God's love. About halfway through my message I became aware that many people had tears flowing down their faces. One of the leaders of the conference sitting behind me, quietly and unobtrusively slipped a note onto the lectern I was using, which read: 'You might like to know that one of the men breaking down with tears running down his face is a notorious attendee of Christian meetings but is known to be argumentative and as hard as nails. God is at work here in a special way.'

That service is one that will live long in my memory. When it was over I wondered as to why it was there were so many tears. I was told, 'We have had so many preachers come to Zimbabwe who have preached at us rather than to us. Some have challenged us and cajoled us and sought to put us right, but as you talked about how much we are loved, we felt all our barriers come down one by one and tears flowed from our hearts simply because they had to – there could be no other adequate response.'

As the blazing sun is set in the heart of this universe and all things revolve around it and have their life from it, so the burning love of God is at the heart of all the life of the Spirit and without it life would be impossible. God can no more stop loving than He can stop living. Nothing can drive the eternal love away. As I said earlier, it is love without condition and it is love without end.

So, if next time you feel a little despairing towards yourself and you think you are not worth being loved and you say, perhaps rather petulantly, 'Lord, why do you keep on loving me?' don't be surprised if

He answers you with 'the strangest, oldest, shortest and most intriguing response in the English language' – Because.

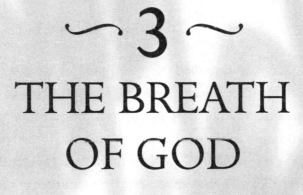

3

THE BREATH
OF GOD

Sermon preached from the pulpit of Moriah Chapel, the place where the 1904 Revival broke out under Evan Roberts. This was the occasion of the 100th anniversary of that great outpouring and was recorded by BBC Wales in May 2004 and later broadcast on the centenary of the outbreak of the Welsh Revival on the morning of 31 October 2004.

JOHN 20:21–22

Again Jesus said, 'Peace be with you! As the Father has sent me, I am sending you.' And with that he breathed on them and said, 'Receive the Holy Spirit.'

Some time ago I went with a friend to see the stage production of C.S. Lewis's great fictional story: *The Lion, the Witch and the Wardrobe* in one of London's theatres. Many of you I am sure are familiar with the plot of how a small group of children go through the back of a wardrobe in an old professor's house and find themselves in a strange and magical land called Narnia.

Its rolling hills, towering mountains and rich, deep forests are populated by the most remarkable beasts, all of whom can speak. Narnia is ruled by a wicked queen who is a usurper to the throne. She is also a witch who is empowered with extraordinary gifts. She is the one who holds Narnia under her spell and part of her curse is to ensure that it was, as Lewis so graphically puts – 'always winter, never Christmas'. The land is covered by snow, cursed by perpetual winter.

A central figure in Lewis's story is the Lion called Aslan. He's a mysterious, wondrous beast who comes from beyond Narnia and beyond time. He's spoken of by others in hushed and awed tones. The Lion figure of course represents Christ and one day lays down his life for Narnia on a stone table, later rising from the dead. After that, wherever he goes, the effects of the curse on Narnia are reversed. The icy rivers begin to thaw, the flowers bud and bloom and there is a whole different atmosphere in the land.

Towards the end of the story, Aslan enters the castle of the wicked queen and finds the courtyard strewn with stone statues. These statues were creatures that had been turned to stone by the curse of the wicked witch. The great beast strides to the first of these statues, lowers his regal head and breathes upon it. As the breath of the Lion touches the stone it ripples into flesh. He does the same to the other statues and one by one they awaken and begin to sing and dance and shout the praises of the one who had turned them from stone to living beings once again.

The scene of Aslan breathing upon the creatures of stone and seeing them spring immediately to life will live forever in my mind. As I watched entranced there came singing into my consciousness the passage we have read from John's Gospel where Jesus is seen breathing upon His disconsolate and dispirited disciples.

Picture this intriguing Bible scene with me again for a moment. It is the period just after Christ's resurrection. The disciples we are told are behind closed doors for fear of the Jews. Bewildered by Christ's death and unable to take in the news that He had come back from the dead it was as if their hearts had turned to stone. Then suddenly, though the doors were shut and locked, the risen Jesus appears in their midst. That must have not just surprised them but left them feeling utterly bewildered and astonished. No wonder His first word to them was 'Peace'; it was as if He were saying, 'Stay calm, everything is under control.' Then after showing them His hands and side and giving them the commission to go and tell the world that He was risen from the dead, He proceeds to breathe all over them.

What a strange thing to do you might think. It is an unwritten law of etiquette that you don't go around breathing on people. How can we account for this peculiar action of Jesus? And what was the purpose of it?

Well consider this. Prior to His death and resurrection Jesus lived like everyone else by breathing in oxygen and breathing out carbon dioxide. But now after His resurrection things are different. He no longer depends on the air of Palestine to support Him. He lives now in the power of an endless life. In His resurrection body He is able to walk through doors, appear and disappear at will. In His new role as the Lord of death and conqueror of the grave I believe it was not the mere exhalation of air that passed between Him and His disciples. It was the energy of eternity; *it was the breath of God.*

I have often wondered to myself what was the reaction of the disciples as Jesus breathed upon them. The Scriptures do not say. Did they feel and experience something or was it, as some believe, simply a symbolic act calculated to prepare them for the mighty outpouring of the Spirit they would receive later on the Day of Pentecost?

Personally, I cannot conceive of Jesus saying 'Receive the Holy Spirit' without the disciples experiencing something being imparted to them. My own view of this strange action of Jesus is that, seeing His perplexed and frightened disciples in need of spiritual support, the opportunity of ministering to them by imparting something of the Spirit's power to their flagging spirits was a foretaste, if you like, of the power that they would receive in much greater measure after Jesus had been glorified.

Some think this was the moment when the disciples were actually converted or born again. Previously all they knew of Jesus was on the other side of the cross. Now, having paid the penalty of sin on the cross and having defeated death, He was in a position to breathe into them the new life that He had won by His victory on Calvary. Whatever He had given them before He was now in a position to give them something more – the regenerating power of the Spirit.

We can only speculate of course on the reason why Jesus breathed on

His disciples, for there is no clear explanation in the passage as to the purpose of that strange action but what I would like to do is to think with you about the various functions of breath. 'Nothing is as intriguing as breathing,' says one medical practitioner and he goes on to say that breath has three distinct functions. I want to borrow the three words he uses to describe the functions of breath and hang upon them my own thoughts concerning this fascinating subject.

FIRST, BREATH *VITALISES*

We can't live without breathing. The rhythm of life is contained in the simple biological fact that we breathe in oxygen and breathe out carbon dioxide. Respiration must be regular. We continue to exist on this earth only as we breathe in and breathe out. When something interferes with our ability to do that then either we get desperately ill or we die.

And the quality of the air we breathe is important also. When I first came to live in London in the early sixties the Clean Air Act had not yet been introduced and often during winter it was impossible to walk the streets because of the dense smog that settled over the city. Sometimes during the winter months the great Metropolis almost came to a standstill as cars and buses were unable to make their way through the densely polluted streets. And those with lung conditions quickly became casualties of the pollution, their lives being brought to a premature end.

Continuing the thought that the quality of the air we breathe is important to our physical vitality, I can remember in my youth in Wales several of my school friends being struck down with tuberculosis. The treatment involved them being removed from the coal mining area in which we lived to sanatoriums built high up in the mountains where the air was purer and free from pollution.

When I asked if I could visit my friends I was told that tuberculosis bacteria spread through inhalation and thus it would be dangerous to come in contact with their breath. In fact I remember a health visitor coming to my school and warning us to keep clear of anyone known to be infected with the disease. I learned that my friends incarcerated in the sanatorium were given breathing exercises and shown how to fill every extremity of their lungs with the purer air.

There is I think a spiritual parallel here. In these days of so many empty and half-empty churches, how desperately we need the *vitalising* breath of God's Spirit to blow over us with the same degree of intensity that He did at Pentecost and at other times in history.

If ever the words of the hymnist 'Breathe on me breath of God, fill me with life anew' deserve not just to be sung once but ought to be constantly on our lips in fervent believing prayer, it is now. Ever since the Day of Pentecost God has breathed His Holy Spirit upon His people and the divine breath has never been taken away. All around us the breath of God is flowing but so many of us are gripped with a kind of spiritual poliomyelitis that our lungs seem to have refused their function. We are like men and women in a gale whose lips are tightly shut because we are afraid to breathe in the life-giving oxygen of the Spirit.

The very first funeral I conducted after I became a minister was that of a little girl who had died with that dreadful disease I just referred to – poliomyelitis. She was just seven years of age, a darling and beautiful girl. I had charge of a church at that time in the small but beautiful town of Llandeilo in Carmarthenshire. Llandeilo is situated in the Towy Valley, a well-known beauty spot where Jeremy Taylor wrote his memoirs. I remember it being a beautiful day and a fresh wind was blowing through the valley as we laid her to rest on one of the slopes. The thought occurred to me as I conducted the funeral and we laid her to rest in the ground that all around was blowing some of the purest and cleanest air in the whole of Wales yet this girl had died because her lungs would not function in the way they were designed.

I once had the joy and privilege of saving a little boy from drowning. My family and I lived for a while in a small community which had its own private swimming pool. I was sitting in my study one morning when my younger son, John, then about eight years of age, rushed in and said, 'Come quickly, Dad, there's a little boy who has been under the water for some time. I think he has drowned.' I hastened to the pool to find the little boy floating beneath the surface. I quickly pulled him out and after turning him over and getting as much water out of his mouth as possible I proceeded to give him what is called 'the kiss of life'. It was a joyous moment I can tell you when I saw his chest begin to move up and down and respiration once again begin. Yes, the good doctor was right – breath vitalises.

SECONDLY, BREATH *STERILISES*

Physiology is not my line. I am more at home in the realm of the soul than of the body. I do have, however, a rudimentary grasp of physiology. Here in my chest slightly inclined to the left is my heart which expands and contracts and every time it does it pumps the blood along my arteries to the extremities of my body. Then it returns, collecting impurities, and when it passes through the lungs it is filtered by the oxygen that we have breathed in and thus cleansed it goes back to the heart where it starts its journey all over again. It is the inhalation of oxygen that keeps our systems clean.

Here again I see another spiritual parallel. I wonder is that what the hymnist was thinking of when he wrote these compelling words: 'Breathe on me breath of God, *until my heart is pure*?'

Day after day we go about our tasks on this sin-stained planet gathering one impurity after another, being forced to listen to blasphemies and language that is an offence both to God and all decent people. Because of this, how we need to breathe in the filtering freshness of the spiritual oxygen that comes to us through His Holy Spirit.

One of the great evidences of the Welsh Revival in 1904 when God's breath blew over the Principality in a powerful way was the fact that people's lives were cleaned up in the most amazing manner. Old debts were paid, bad language gave way to the praises of God and people would cross the valleys to each other's homes in order to clear up any bad feeling that had been between them.

It was like this in the Hebrides Revival in 1959 too. A group of people were praying in church and some stood up and read from Psalm 24: 'Who may ascend the hill of the LORD? Who may stand in his holy place? He who has clean hands and a pure heart, who does not lift up his soul to an idol or swear by what is false' (vv.3–4).

One of the congregation followed the reading with a prayer that went something like this: 'O God, forgive us if our hands are not clean and our hearts are not pure.' A young man immediately stood up and startled the congregation by crying out: 'It is so much humbug to talk about our hands and hearts not being clean. We need to drop the "our" and replace it with "my".'

Then he proceeded to pray, 'Oh God, my hands are not clean, my heart is not pure ... forgive me...' and falling to the ground in repentance provoked others to follow in the same vein. People made their praying very personal and cried out to God in such a way that the Holy Spirit fell on the island ushering in one of the great movements of the Spirit in the twentieth century.

Returning if I may for a moment to the 1904 Revival, which we are celebrating today, one of the characteristics of that revival, when God breathed over Wales in such tremendous spiritual power, was the fact that morality was lifted to a higher level. People touched by the Revival began to live cleaner and more righteous lives. Those who had stolen things returned them to their rightful owners. It is a well-known fact that miners who directed the pit ponies with swear words, after they were converted didn't want to swear anymore, so they had to teach the pit ponies new and cleaner commands.

The Welsh words for Holy Spirit are *Ysbryd Glan* – the clean Spirit. What a beautiful expression. If God were to breathe again over Wales in the way He did in 1904 I can promise you that we would have a cleaner and more moral society. Revival would drastically reduce sleaze, pay off old debts, clean up our language, reduce sexual immorality and restore to Wales once again a sense of destiny. Breath sterilises.

THIRDLY, BREATH *VOCALISES*

Do you realise it takes breath to give birth to speech? You may have a perfect voice box, your epiglottis may be a model of muscular elasticity, but I can promise you if there is no breath, there will be no sound. It is breath passing through the voice box that produces the sounds we call speech.

On the Day of Pentecost we are told the disciples were all filled with the Spirit and began to *speak* ... They were men and women with new voices. The same Spirit enabled the vacillating disciple Simon Peter to stand up and preach a sermon that convinced 3,000 people to become followers of Jesus Christ. Just imagine it – one sermon and 3,000 people are won to Christ. Nowadays, even with the same Spirit available to us, in some places it takes 3,000 sermons to win one soul to Christ!

Christians, someone has said, are like trumpets; they are not much good until breath is blown into them. Certainly the breath of God that blew over Wales in 1904 caused thousands of men and women to lift their voices in praise and glory to God. They would pray and sing God's praises for hours and miners could be heard singing the great hymns of the faith in the cages that carried them from the pit bottom to the surface.

It's wonderful to hear some of those hymns still being sung at football matches but how much more wonderful it would be to see churches filled with men and women who were vocal for God both in both prayer and praise.

The great John Wesley when he lay dying in the East End of London was said to lament the fact that he could no longer travel on horseback across the land using his lungs to preach the glorious gospel of Jesus Christ. It is reported that he said to one of the friends who visited him: 'My breath is almost gone, but I am content in the knowledge that the breath God gave me has been used in presenting Christ to the people.' Then just before he died I understand he lifted himself up on the pillow and began to sing:

> I'll praise my Maker while I've breath
> And when my voice is lost in death,
> Praise shall employ my nobler powers,
> My days of praise shall ne'er be past
> While life and thought and being last
> And immortality endures.

After that Wesley drew his last breath on this earth. But he is singing still. Will we be able to breathe in heaven? Will we have lungs? It is impossible to say, but here on this earth how important it is for us to use our breath to proclaim Christ in all His glory and splendour.

We have many needs in Wales but I believe with all my heart that our greatest need is for another visitation from heaven that will stir all Christians and bring those who do not yet know Him into a personal relationship with God and His Son Jesus Christ.

Join me, if you will, in a prayer that God's vitalising, sterilising, vocalising breath will blow over again as He did in the days past.

PRAYER

Lord Jesus, risen ascended and glorified, blow over our land once again with the breath of Your Spirit. Give us another Pentecost at any cost. Let this land which in times past has been shaken by the power of Your Spirit and seen multitudes brought into Your kingdom witness once more the moving of Your Spirit as in olden days. Breathe, Holy Spirit, once again on Wales and other parts of the United Kingdom, indeed the whole world, for unless You do our nation is in peril. In Christ's peerless and most powerful name we ask it. Amen.

4

HE'S JUST A CARPENTER

MARK 6:1–3

Rarely do I take a text for a sermon from the Living Bible for, delightful though it is, it is more a paraphrase than a direct translation. However on this occasion I believe it captures the mood of a certain situation that took place in the life of Jesus in a clear and most beautiful way. And because of that, I would like you to read carefully these words rather than looking them up in your own translation.

> Soon afterwards he left that section of the country and returned with his disciples to Nazareth, his home town. The next Sabbath he went to the synagogue to teach, and the people were astonished at his wisdom and his miracles because he was just a local man like themselves.
>
> 'He's no better than we are,' they said. 'He's just a carpenter, Mary's boy ...'

Several times in the Gospels we come across what might be described as 'unintentional tributes' – statements made about our Lord that were intended to be humiliating and demeaning but when looked at from another perspective appear in a completely different light.

Take this for example: 'While Jesus was having dinner at Matthew's house, many tax collectors and "sinners" came and ate with him and his disciples. When the Pharisees saw this, they asked his disciples, "Why does your teacher eat with tax collectors and 'sinners'?"' (Matt. 9:10–11).

The fact that Jesus ate with tax collectors and sinners offended the

Pharisees and their words were meant as a slur, but actually that was one of the greatest things about Jesus – though He was the Lord of Glory yet He condescended to rub shoulders with sinners.

It was an unintentional tribute.

Then what about this: As He hung upon the cross some of the onlookers said about Him: 'He saved others ... but he can't save himself!' (Matt. 27:42). It was said in a demeaning manner but again looked at from another perspective the fact that He did not save Himself was another great thing about Him. He could have saved Himself; by not doing so He saved us. Another unintentional tribute.

And the verse I want to take as my text – He's just a carpenter, Mary's boy' – could be put in the same category. The words, too, were said derisively, contemptuously and were intended to demean the Saviour. But those who said this about Him were paying Him another unintentional tribute. For they would come to see that this humble carpenter built much more than doors or ploughs or yokes, He re-built the lives of those who, stained by sin, yielded to His claims.

Though the statement: 'He's just a carpenter' was not meant as a compliment, it was one of the most interesting and intriguing things they could have said about our Lord.

Let me tell you why.

It was no mere coincidence, I think, that Christ was a carpenter. He might have been so many other things – a farmer, a fisherman or a builder. But no, He was a carpenter. And the more I think about it the more I find a sublime fitness in that fact. For a carpenter makes things. Barns, children's toys, doors, tables, chairs. Jesus as a carpenter must have made them all. I wonder what He charged for chairs in Nazareth! Long before He was crucified to a cross and the nails held the Carpenter, the Carpenter held the nails. I wonder as He hammered the nails into wood

– did He realise that one day men would hammer nails into Him.

In a sense Jesus was a carpenter, a maker of things *before* He came to Nazareth. 'Through him,' says the Gospel writer John, 'all things were made, without him nothing was made that has been made' (John 1:3). He who wielded axe and plane and hammer in the tiny village of Nazareth once laid down the timbers of the universe.

And He was a maker too *after* He left Nazareth. When the day came that He took off His apron for the last time, put away His tools and closed the door of the carpenter's shop behind Him for ever, He did not cease to be a carpenter. Only His materials were different. He worked not with wood but with men and women. The wood worker became a wonder worker, transforming the lives of men and women. And to His disciples He said, 'Follow me and I will *make* you fishers of men' (Matt. 4:19, my italics).

One of the joys on my travels to the Holy Land has been to preach in the chapel of the Christian hospital high up on the hill overlooking the little village of Nazareth. The pulpit in the chapel is built in the shape of a carpenter's bench. I can't begin to tell you the emotions that have swept through me a number of times as I have stood behind that carpenter's bench and preached to the various groups of pilgrims who love to visit the chapel.

On one occasion my colleague Trevor Partridge and I conducted a week-long seminar in the hospital for the doctors and nurses and often I would slip into the chapel to be on my own and reflect on the fact that it was here in Nazareth that Jesus spent His youth and worked as a carpenter. It was while sitting there in the chapel all alone one day that these thoughts I am about to share with you now came to me.

I want to suggest three things about this Carpenter of Nazareth that causes Him to be such a wonder.

Firstly – He is a Carpenter who selects the most unlikely materials. Most carpenters like to select the best wood they can when making something. But not this one. Just look at the disciples He chose, for example. What a motley bunch they were.

I once did a study of the 12 disciples and I came to the conclusion that they represented all the points of the psychological compass. There was Simon Peter, bluff, blundering, arrogant, impetuous, even foul-mouthed at times. Then there was Judas, the betrayer, whose heart became open to Satan. The disciple Matthew had been a tax gatherer, the type of person who was hated by the Jews. When you look at the other disciples there doesn't seem much to qualify them to become the future leaders of the world's greatest enterprise – the Christian Church. But Jesus does not hesitate to enrol them in His school of discipleship.

If there is one thing I have noticed in my long life it is that Christ does not always choose the well adjusted, the best educated or the sophisticated to accomplish His purposes. When I was doing my counsellor training in the USA many years ago I went to listen to one of America's leading secular counsellors – Rollo May – who said that the best counsellors are not always those who are well-adjusted personalities.

That was a great relief to me I can tell you because I had just undergone a battery of psychological tests and I hadn't come out of them too well! Along with Rollo May's statement I found the words of the apostle Paul also encouraging: 'But we have this treasure in jars of clay to show that this all-surpassing power is from God and not from us' (2 Cor. 4:7).

When I left the first church I pastored in the little town of Helston, Cornwall, a lady gave me a present of a pair of beautifully carved doves. I asked, 'How long did it take you to make these?'

'It took me about three weeks,' she said, 'but it took me three years to find the wood'. She told me how she used to go down to the harbour every day in Porthleven and look for wood that had been washed up by the tide.

'The grain is so beautiful', I said, 'why is that so?'

'Ah', she said, 'you should have seen it when I found it. It was all bent and gnarled and twisted but that's the kind of wood that produces the most spectacular grain.'

It has always interested me that people whose lives have gone through the mill as we say and who seem to be bent and twisted out of shape can be touched by Christ in such a wonderful way that they contribute powerfully to the lives of others. A Christian woman I have known for many years and whom I once had the privilege of counselling has an amazing ministry amongst young people who have suffered great physical or sexual abuse in their developmental years.

When she first told me of the abuse she had gone through as a child I found it almost impossible to believe. Yet there was clear evidence to support it. At the age of 12 she went into deep depression and remained in that state for ten years, depending on antidepressants just to get through the day. During our counselling sessions she met Christ in a most wonderful way and her life was turned completely around. Within months she was ministering to others with such sensitivity and skill that those of us who watched her grow and share the life that Christ had put within her with others found it almost too good to be true.

One of my colleagues in the church I then pastored, visited me in my home and during the course of conversation asked me how it could be that a woman with such a history of abuse and mistreatment could function in such a way. 'She is so amazing', he said, 'I can't understand how a woman with such a history could rise to such rich levels of ministry – and in such a short time.'

I pointed him to the doves given to me when I left my first church that were sitting on my mantle shelf and told him how the woman who had carved them for me had searched for three years for wood that was misshapen and twisted and gnarled because it was that kind of wood that produced the most spectacular grain. 'That woman,' I said, 'has gone through the hands of the Carpenter of Nazareth, and has come out as a testimony to His awesome and wonderful changing power.'

So often throughout the years I have been in the Christian ministry I have seen those who have suffered the most terrible circumstances and situations rise to become valiant warriors in the service of Jesus Christ. I have learned that the man or woman who has every advantage is not always the person to envy. Those who get everything they want sometimes get something they don't want, either an unsympathetic hardness of heart or a dangerous flaw in the will. The absence of advantage such as a poor education, or a physical or mental disability, does not disqualify us from being used by Jesus Christ.

Christian history is replete with people who in their early years lacked the benefits of a loving home, a good education, a fertile mind and so on, but they learned that there is power with God to turn stumbling blocks into stepping stones. The apostle Paul in 1 Corinthians 1:27–29 said: 'But God chose the foolish things of the world to shame the wise; God chose the weak things of the world to shame the strong. He chose the lowly things of this world and the despised things – and the things that are not – to nullify the things that are, so that no-one may boast before him.'

Secondly – the Carpenter of Nazareth not only selects the most unlikely materials but spends time carefully shaping and fashioning them. Whether we are unlikely material or not, every one of us once selected has to be shaped. And the shaping process is not easy to bear, but it has to be done. How do you respond to the shaping process I wonder? The Carpenter of Nazareth puts you on His bench, and the plane, the saw and the chisel go to work and as He comes up against the knots and the flaws, soon the shivers of wood fly in all directions. Often it is not a pleasant experience when God shapes us for service in His kingdom, but we will not be able to arrive at our full potential without it.

There is an old saying that though God loves us as we are He loves us too much to let us stay as we are, and He works on us in ways that sometimes we wish He loved us less. St Augustine, one of the early Church Fathers, discovered this when God began to work in his life and such were the challenges he went through that one day he cried out: 'O Lord love me less.'

C.S. Lewis described this process as the 'Intolerable Compliment'. Here are His words:

Over a sketch made idly to amuse a child an artist may not take too much trouble; he may be content to let it go, even though it is not exactly as he meant it to be. But over the great picture of his life – the work which he loves – he will take endless trouble and would doubtless, therefore, give endless trouble to the picture if it were sentient. One can imagine a sentient picture, after being rubbed and scraped and re-commenced for the tenth time, wishing that it were only a thumbnail sketch whose making was over in a minute. In the same way it is natural for us to wish that God designed us for a less glorious and arduous destiny, but then we are wishing not for more love but less. Our hearts cry out for a loving God. Well the truth is we have one. His love however will not allow us to remain less than we can be.[1]

Christ sees in us more than we can see in ourselves and will work to bring that out. Many years ago a sculptor by the name of Andrew Borgum was commissioned to make a wood carving of the head of Abraham Lincoln. There was an African-American maid cleaning the rooms and she watched the sculptor at work day after day chiselling and chipping away, and then one day it was finished. The maid in astonishment seeing the finished work ran to the housekeeper in terror and said, 'Is that Mr Lincoln's head?'

'Yes,' said the housekeeper.

The maid thought for a moment and then blurted out, 'How did Mr Borgum know that Mr Lincoln's head was in that block of wood?'

How did Jesus know that Peter the Rock was in Peter the unstable? How did He know that Paul the apostle was in Saul the persecutor? Because He sees with a double vision. A carpenter understands this principle you see. Jesus as a carpenter could see a table in a block of wood, or even a child's toy or something of beauty.

And He carried that principle over into His work with men and women. He looked at them with a double vision. He could see things as they were but also as they could be. He could see heaven in a mustard seed, He could see the Church in a loaf of bread, He could see faith in the trustfulness of a little child, and He could see disciples hidden in fishermen.

As Jesus worked with people He encountered knots and faults but His plane and chisel and sandpaper shaped them to become what they were. It required infinite patience but He continues to work on us.

Many years ago on one of my visits to the United States I came across hundreds of Christians wearing badges which had on it these initials: PBPWMGHFWMY. At first I was puzzled and, asking someone what they meant, I was told – *Please Be Patient With Me God Hasn't Finished*

With Me Yet! How important it is that we grasp that simple but sublime truth.

Peter the unstable didn't become Peter the Rock on the basis of a one-hour conversation with Jesus. It took time and patience on His part. There are some things Christ can do instantly. He could give a blind man sight – instantly. He could turn water into wine – instantly. He could bring the dead to life – instantly. But it takes time to make a saint. A person said to me on one occasion, 'I wish I had never been made.'

'My dear,' I said, 'you haven't been made; you are still under construction.'

Thirdly, the Carpenter of Nazareth not only selects the most unlikely materials, and carefully shapes them but He also sanctifies them and sets them aside for His purpose. The word 'sanctified' has several meanings; it means dedication, separation and cleansing. The vessels in the ancient tabernacle had to be set apart specifically for God's use. In the same way, God wants us not simply to decorate His world but to change it. He wants to use us. He desires to set us apart to that special purpose He has for every single one of us.

Before we were formed in our mother's womb He saw us and planned our destiny. And He has led every one of us through the labyrinth of the years to this very moment. Everything He has allowed in our lives has been because He foresaw how He could turn it to good and work to refining our characters, deepening our sensitivity to Himself and sharpening our effectiveness in His service.

He works with us so that we may work with others. And just as He never stops working with us we must never stop working with others, praying for them, investing our lives in them.

In the early days of my ministry I asked God to make me a counsellor and it was not long after that I began to experience all kinds of problems and difficulties. One day I prayed: 'Lord, what are you doing to me?' I felt I was being bent out of shape but the thought arose in my mind, put there by the Holy Spirit I believe: 'You asked to be a counsellor, and this is part of My purpose for you too. In being set apart for this you need to feel My comfort in your struggles so that you will be able to comfort others in their struggles.' The following text sprang into my mind at that moment:

> Praise be to the God and Father of our Lord Jesus Christ, the Father of compassion and the God of all comfort, who comforts us in all our troubles, so that we can comfort those in any trouble with the comfort we ourselves have received from God.
>
> 2 Cor. 1:3–4

Nowadays as I look back over my life, something I do frequently, I view the times of difficulty, the doubts, the trials, the reverses, betrayals, and I thank God for every one of them. I have learned more from the hours of suffering than from the moments of triumph. I am so glad that the people God uses and chooses are not always the great, the well adjusted, the sophisticates; but people like you and me, ordinary, unlikely material on whom He lavishes His love and grace. Blessed be His holy name.

I have always loved these lines from the pen of George MacDonald, the great Christian writer of a past day and generation. Listen carefully to them.

> I pray O Master let me lie
> As on thy bench the favoured wood

Thy saw, thy plane, thy chisel fly
Make me into something beautiful – and good.

Whether you are young, middle aged or in your senior years, Jesus Christ wants to use you at every point of your life here on earth. Whatever your ambitions or desires to be used in His service, remember He is out there striding ahead of you and He is looking back over His shoulder and saying to you, 'Come on ... Follow me ... I will *make* you ... I *will make you* ... into someone whose service for Me will bring great glory to My name'.

The people of our Lord's village, Nazareth, said, 'He's just a carpenter. Mary's boy'. *Just* a carpenter? Little did they realise it but that Carpenter would go on to take the wood of the cross and make out of it so many things – a ladder that reaches from earth to heaven, a coffin in which to bury our sin, and a throne from which He rules in our hearts.

So words that were said contemptuously, derisively and sarcastically by the people of Nazareth, come over to those of us who know Him in a completely different light.

'He's just a carpenter.'

Just a carpenter?

Just a carpenter?

My response is – What a carpenter!

What a carpenter!

NOTE

1. C.S. Lewis, *The Problem with Pain* (Fount, 1998).

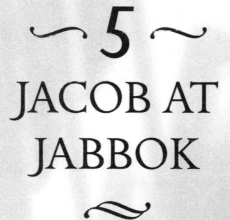

~ 5 ~

JACOB AT JABBOK

That night Jacob got up and took his two wives, his two maidservants and his eleven sons and crossed the ford of the Jabbok. After he had sent them across the stream, he sent over all his possessions. So Jacob was left alone, and a man wrestled with him till daybreak. When the man saw that he could not overpower him, he touched the socket of Jacob's hip so that his hip was wrenched as he wrestled with the man. Then the man said, 'Let me go, for it is daybreak.'

But Jacob replied, 'I will not let you go unless you bless me.'

The man asked him, 'What is your name?'

'Jacob,' he answered.

Then the man said, 'Your name will no longer be Jacob, but Israel, because you have struggled with God and with men and have overcome.'

Jacob said, 'Please tell me your name.'

But he replied, 'Why do you ask my name?' Then he blessed him there.

So Jacob called the place Peniel, saying, 'It is because I saw God face to face, and yet my life was spared.' (vv.22–30)

There is a lot of talk nowadays in evangelical circles about the need to wrestle with principalities and powers. Some of the bestselling books in the Christian market are those that tell us how to do combat with the devil and how to overcome the dark demons that seek to sabotage the efforts of God's people.

There is of course a place for what is called 'spiritual warfare' and I have nothing to say against it. In some ways it's kind of exciting to wrestle with principalities and powers because when we link ourselves with an all-powerful God we are always on the winning side. But the wrestling I want to talk about now is not wrestling with the powers of darkness but *wrestling with God*. This kind of wrestling is mostly always painful, sometimes extremely debilitating and, it has to be said, when we wrestle with God – we always lose! But it is in wrestling with Him I believe that we become truly authentic people, that we leave our false selves and touch reality. When we pit our weight against God and He pits His weight against us – and pins us to the mat – then something happens, if we respond correctly, that brings about great changes in our characters and in our personalities.

One of the greatest examples we have in Scripture of wrestling with God is to be found in the passage we have just read. I refer of course to the patriarch, Jacob. Permit me to give you a thumbnail biographical sketch of this fascinating Old Testament character.

A TUSSLE IN THE WOMB

Jacob, as no doubt you know, was a twin, the other being his brother Esau. Rebekah his mother was weary with a long pregnancy and we are told that the twins fought in the womb. When they were born, Esau came first and Jacob second. The Scriptures say that Jacob had his hand on his brother's heel. If you will allow me to indulge in a little imagination for a moment I can picture Rebekah saying to the midwife, 'What is taking so long?' and the midwife replying, 'The first one is hung up by his foot and your next baby is trying to pull him back in!'

After they were born the midwife probably said to Rebekah: 'What are you going to name these boys? The answer came: Big Red and Heel Grabber. That I think would be a fair modern day translation of the names Esau and Jacob.

Little Heel Grabber was unhappy right from the start. He hated being born second. When you lose a race down the birth canal you end up wanting to compensate for it. By his late teens Heel Grabber would swindle his brother out of his birthright, and feed his old blind father a goat just to get his blessing. As a result of all this Esau swore that he would kill Jacob.

Jacob left the country and went to Haran. On his way there he had an encounter with God when he dreamed he saw a ladder between heaven and earth. He awoke and vowed that the eternal God would be his God and that he would give Him a tenth of all he possessed. He had a kind of half conversion. He would give a tenth but not himself; Jacob the supplanter was still intact. He met God but he did not allow that meeting to produce deep changes in his life.

THE CHEATER GETS CHEATED

In Haran, he met up with his uncle Laban and agreed to work for him for seven years if he could have Laban's beautiful daughter Rachel to be his wife. After the seven years was up and the wedding day arrived Jacob was in for a big surprise. The cheater got cheated. When Laban handed over his veiled daughter to Jacob for their first night together he discovered in the light of the morning that the woman he had slept with was not Rachel but Leah!

When you build up a false world around you by your own falseness then it is not surprising that people turn false to you. One psychologist says: 'You sooner or later get into the environment suitable to your inner attitudes – you build your outer world out of your inner world.

The honest man and woman often begets honesty around them. The inner and the outer tend to coalesce.'

Disappointed but undaunted, Jacob made an agreement with Laban that he would work another seven years for Rachel and during those seven years he developed a plan on how to pay back Laban for his cunning and deceit. The details of the story can be found in the chapter prior to the passage from which I have taken my text. When finally he had been given Rachel to be his wife, he one night rustled a herd of cows and took off under cover of darkness. Laban soon discovered this and Jacob, just as he had fled from Esau, now had to flee from Laban.

But in running away from Laban he found that he was running into Esau. The peril he faced from his angry uncle was as nothing compared to the peril he faced in relation to his angry brother. And when we come upon him in the passage which we have just read, we see him engaged in desperate prayer. He sent his wives and children across the ford at Jabbok about 20 miles north of the Dead Sea. There at the brook Jabbok he was alone – like an animal caught in a trap.

It is clear that he must deal with some things in his life and very soon if he is to survive. He is at the point of desperation. Perhaps we might pause here to make the point that sometimes in life we have to deal with our past before we can have a future. Just as the River Severn separates England from Wales so often the past and the future are separated not by a huge river but a tiny stream which we might call Jabbok. Jabbok is a place of honesty, of repentance, of authenticity.

A WRESTLING MATCH WITH A DIFFERENCE

Whilst at the brook Jabbok and beset by fear and trepidation there appeared to Jacob a man who began to wrestle with Him. It is difficult to know exactly who this 'man' was, but all commentators agree that he was a divine provision. Some believe him to be an angel in the form of a man. Some believe him to be a theophany – a pre-incarnation appearance of Christ. Whoever it was, there can be no doubt the encounter was a divine appointment – the eternal God was behind it all.

As the man wrestled with Jacob, the patriarch became more and more desperate. Perhaps he knew that this was his moment to be changed. I infer that from the fact that Jacob clung to the 'man' in desperation. And when the 'man' touched his hip, put it out of joint and said, 'Now let me go'. Jacob replies, 'No I will not let you go until you bless me'. Jacob had received a blessing from his father by trickery but that blessing had been vitiated by Jacob's ugly and unbecoming behaviour. Was he now ready to be through with all pretence and unreality? Was he ready to wrestle until he found release from himself and the predicaments his crooked self had got him into?

Let me pause here once more to ask the question: Are you desperate for deep spiritual change in your life? So desperate perhaps that you feel if it doesn't happen soon then you worry for your spiritual future? Then let me as God's servant and representative tell you that what happened to Jacob can well happen to you today. Follow me closely as I lead you through the next few fascinating steps.

At one point in the fierce wrestling match the 'man' said to Jacob, 'What is your name?' What might be the significance of that? Well, in Bible days, names were not just designations, but descriptions. Often, when a person's character was changed, his or her name was changed also. Saul of Tarsus was changed to Paul the apostle, for example. Jacob's name as we know meant supplanter, deceiver, opportunist, heel grabber. The 'man' then said, 'Your name will no longer be Jacob, but Israel, because you have struggled with God and with men and have overcome'. In and through that wrestling match the crooked Jacob would be made straight and, as we know, it was by this name that the great nation of the Jews (the Israelites) would come to be named.

The admission by Jacob of his name was deeply important. He had to come to a place of self-awareness and self-understanding if he were to move on into a new future. We can never change what we won't acknowledge and the moment Jacob admitted his name, and all that was gathered up in that name, he was on his way to a new future and a new relationship with God.

'My name is Jacob,' he said, implying of course, a supplanter, a cheat and a crook. The depths were uncovered. Jacob's soul was naked before God. The real man was up and out. This was his most honest moment. He had hit rock bottom.

If you have not reached that place, you will have to stop everything and say this one thing to God – your name. It will be hard to get that name out, you may even choke on it. But get it out, no matter the cost, for there is no new name until you say the old name. The saying of the old name is a confession – a catharsis.

AN UGLY MOMENT IN MY OWN MINISTRY

How many of you, I wonder, have had a wrestling match with God similar to the one Jacob experienced? I have had a few in my time. One of the most significant I ever experienced took place after I had been in the ministry just a few years.

I preached a sermon one night in the church of which I was a pastor, that was so filled with theological terms and phrases that it went right over the heads of the congregation. I did this not because I wanted to bless or encourage the people but to impress them with my knowledge of theology. It was an ugly moment in my ministry.

The passage I preached from was Philippians chapter 2 where Paul talks about the descent of Christ from heaven to earth. Here were the three points on which I hung my sermon: Pleromatic divinity; Pleromatic humanity; Hypostatic union.

After I had finished the sermon a friend of mine, who was a professor in a nearby university, took me aside and said, 'I think that is one of the most brilliant sermons I have ever heard. I think you are more brilliant than Einstein.' I remember feeling somewhat superior to other mortals at that remark – after all Einstein and his Theory of Relativity was being talked about almost everywhere at that time – and to be compared to Einstein inflated my ego almost to cosmic proportions.

My friend paused for a moment and, looking me directly in the eye, said, 'Yes, it is believed that there are only about twelve people in the world who can understand Einstein; *I doubt whether anyone can understand you!*'

I felt stunned for a moment as I realised he had set me up to bring me down. Turning to his Bible he read me these words from Proverbs 27:6: 'Faithful are the wounds of a friend' (AV). 'Look,' he said, 'I love you too much to let you get away with this. Your message went right over the heads of these people. Remember that Jesus said "Feed my sheep", not "Feed my giraffes"! I am going to pray that God will help you overcome this tendency you have to show off your ability with words and make you a true shepherd of souls.' He then turned on his heels and walked off.

That conversation put me off my food for three days and I spent them kneeling before God asking Him to change me in the way I needed to be changed. I wrestled with God and cried out to Him over and over again, 'God, I need to change; how do I begin? What can I do about this tendency to show off and impress people with my words?'

Then God did to me what he did with Jacob. He said, 'What is your name?' I resisted answering the question for a long time. I threw my whole weight against Him but at last I had to say it. I had to spit it out. I almost choked on it. What was my name?

It was *Ego*!

I was more interested in boosting my self-esteem and self-worth by impressing people than ministering to them in the humility which ought to be characteristic of every servant of God.

Then God did the same to me that He did to Jacob; He touched something inside me that instantly crippled me. I felt my ego receive a blow that made me inwardly wince. I walk with a limp now. Oh you can't see it in my stride; it's in my soul.[1] I am badly crippled; I can't walk without support – His support. The spirit of independence was broken that day and now I never get up to preach or sit down to write without saying, 'Lord, help me not to be caught up in an odious attempt to impress people but help me to bless them.'

So I ask you again: What about you? Ever had a wrestling match with God? Perhaps you don't need to. Perhaps you are not ready to; but if you are, then take it from me He will ask you your name. And as I said earlier you will have to say your old name before you get a new name.

A TIME TO GET PERSONAL

Let's assume however that many of those of you hearing me at this moment are ready for a wrestling match with the Almighty. You are tired of the way your spiritual life is going and you have come today to the brook Jabbok and you are desperate for change, desperate to meet with God.

What is your name?

Perhaps it is one of the following:

Resentment – you are eaten up with bitterness which you will not let go of.

Negativity – you are always saying No

Self-pity – you are caught in the 'poor me' syndrome and you focus on how unfortunate you are.

Inferiority – you see yourself as a person of no worth, even though you are a joint heir with Christ.

Pride – your soul is stiff and starched and shot through with an unwillingness to humble yourself.

Guilt – there are huge moral and spiritual violations in your life that you haven't asked forgiveness for.

Hypocrisy – you are one thing in secret another thing in public.

Conflict – your soul is a civil war.

Just say your name. Remember Jabbok is a place of honesty. God will change your name

From resentment to forgiveness
From fear to faith
From gloom to glad-heartedness
From defeat to victory
From barrenness to fruitfulness
From negativism to positivism
From all that is wrong to all that is right.

I said earlier that every time we wrestle with God we lose. But in the losing we find a new spiritual understanding that sets us up for a new relationship with God and a new dependency upon Him. In the struggle we become more authentic, more real.

A CHANGE IN US BRINGS ABOUT CHANGE IN OTHERS

When something happened to Jacob something happened around him. It was not long after that wrestling match that he looked into the distance and saw Esau coming towards him – the brother who had sworn to kill him. But God had changed the heart of Esau and he ran and embraced Jacob.

The passage is so moving I think that rather than trying to paraphrase it, I would like us to read it straight from Scripture:

> But Esau ran to meet Jacob and embraced him; he threw his arms around his neck and kissed him. And they wept. Then Esau looked up and saw the women and children. 'Who are these with you?' he asked.
>
> Jacob answered, 'They are the children God has graciously given your servant.'
>
> Then the maidservants and their children approached and bowed down. Next, Leah and her children came and bowed down. Last of all came Joseph and Rachel, and they too bowed down.
>
> Esau asked, 'What do you mean by all these droves I met?'
>
> 'To find favour in your eyes, my lord,' he said.
>
> But Esau said, 'I already have plenty, my brother. Keep what you have for yourself.'
>
> Gen. 33:4–9

How true it is that 'When a man's ways please the LORD, He makes even his enemies to be at peace with him' (Prov. 16:7, NKJV).

Just before we leave the story of Jacob the question needs to be asked: How deep was the change that God wrought in the patriarch? Well, turn with me to Genesis 35:1–7, and note what it says:

Then God said to Jacob, 'Go up to Bethel and settle there, and build an altar there to God, who appeared to you when you were fleeing from your brother Esau.'

So Jacob said to his household and to all who were with him, 'Get rid of the foreign gods you have with you, and purify yourselves and change your clothes. Then come, let us go up to Bethel, where I will build an altar to God, who answered me in the day of my distress and who has been with me wherever I have gone.' So they gave Jacob all the foreign gods they had and the rings in their ears, and Jacob buried them under the oak at Shechem. Then they set out, and the terror of God fell upon the towns all around them so that no-one pursued them.

Jacob and all the people with him came to Luz (that is, Bethel) in the land of Canaan. There he built an altar, and he called the place El Bethel, because it was there that God revealed himself to him when he was fleeing from his brother.

The great changes that had begun in Jacob sent a moral tide through his people also. When God changes us He can also change others through us. Keep that thought ever in your mind.

It may be that as you go through life you might have several wrestling matches with the Lord. Rarely are we perfected by just one encounter. That has been my experience and it may well be your experience also.

Several times in my life I have come to Jabbok and I hear myself saying, 'Here we are again Lord.' Do I shrink from these experiences? Oh no. I need the reality they produce. The bell rings and we come out of our corners – God and me. We wrestle and I lose. I throw my weight against Him and He throws His weight against me and touches some part of me that needs crippling. He throws me to the mat. But I am a joyous loser because to lose to God is to win in life. It means you will walk with a limp.

Some of you may walk away today to face a wrestling match with the Almighty. Don't be afraid. You may walk with a limp thereafter but you will come to know in a deeper way than ever before the truth of Christ's words: '... without me you can do nothing' (John 15:5, NKJV).

NOTE

1. When I first preached this sermon I did not have a physical limp but prostate cancer which spread into my right leg has changed that. I now walk with a limp both spiritually and physically.

6
CONSTRAINED!

2 CORINTHIANS 5:14

For the love of Christ constrains us, because we judge thus: that if one died for all, then all died; and he died for all, that those who live should live no longer for themselves, but for him who died for them and rose again. (NKJV)

There are times it seems in the New Testament when the pen of the apostle Paul catches fire – and nowhere is that more evident than in the chapter before us.

Paul has been arguing – and to my mind, arguing magnificently – for the Christian's indebtedness to Christ and although usually the apostle's language is orderly and precise, here for a moment his language shakes itself free of all restraint and in a moment of flaming certainty unfolds for us what ought to be the driving force behind everything we do – the all-consuming and constraining love of Christ.

All commentators agree we are closer to Paul's heart in 2 Corinthians than in any of his other epistles. Here he opens up his heart to his readers in a way he does not do in his other letters. If you want to get close to Paul's mind read the epistle to the Romans. There you get a glimpse of his magisterial thinking, and as you follow the twists and turns of his arguments you cannot help but get the idea you are in touch with a most marvellous intellect indeed.

But in 2 Corinthians he opens up his heart to us in the most personal of ways and lets us glimpse, albeit for a moment, something of the passion that burns within him.

I have chosen to take my text from one of the early editions of the New King James Version because it uses the word 'constrains' – an old English word that for me has a better feel about it than the word found in other translations such as 'compels' or 'controls'. In fact the newer editions of the New King James Version substitute 'compels' for 'constrains' – a mistake in my estimation.

As a writer and a preacher words are the tools of my trade. I have loved words ever since I came across them. I am fascinated by the way one word will strike the imagination in a way that a similar word will not. Mark Twain said 'the difference between the right word and the almost right word is the difference between a lightning flash and a firefly'.

Sometimes when I am writing I will spend several minutes looking for the right word as opposed to the almost right word. There is tremendous power in words.

I was fascinated when studying this text some time ago to discover that the original Greek word which is translated 'constrains', 'controls', or 'compels' is a word that Paul uses only twice in the whole of his writings. The Greek word is *sunecho* and is used on only two occasions by the apostle Paul, here in 2 Corinthians 5:14 and in Philippians 1:23 where he talks about being torn (*sunecho*) between two things, the desire to stay and continue his ministry on earth and his desire to depart and be with Christ.

The word really is a medical word and that is why in nine out of its twelve occurrences in the New Testament it is used by Dr Luke. In order that we might understand something of what might have been in Paul's mind when he made the statement 'the love of Christ *constrains* us' let me select just three passages in Luke's Gospel where he uses the word. These three passages will I believe act like a window letting in some light on what Paul was trying to say when he wrote in 2 Corinthians 5:14, 'the love of Christ constrains us.'

Take first this passage from Luke 4:38–39:

Jesus left the synagogue and went to the home of Simon. Now Simon's mother-in-law was suffering from a high fever, and they asked Jesus to help her. So he bent over her and rebuked the fever, and it left her. She got up at once and began to wait on them.

The word 'suffering' is a translation of the word *sunecho*. Other translations render it as 'taken', or 'afflicted', or as Eugene Peterson in *The Message* puts it: 'she was running a high fever'. We could also say, quite justifiably, that she was 'constrained' by a great fever.

Picture the scene with me. Peter's wife's mother was sick. Some dreaded germ of the East had got into her bloodstream, pushed up her temperature and now she was burning up with a raging fever. When Jesus arrived at Simon Peter's home He was asked to help her whereupon He ministered to her and immediately she was healed.

I don't know if you have ever seen anyone with a raging fever; it can be a very unnerving sight. I remember on one occasion ministering in the little town of Kisumu on the Equator in East Africa, when a friend of mine asked me if I would go with him to pray for his father who lived out in the bush and was desperately sick with a high fever. We trekked for an hour or so through the bush and came eventually to a rather primitive hut where the old man lived. When I got inside and my eyes grew accustomed to the half light (there were no windows, just the light that streamed in from the open door), I saw a sight that quite staggered me. The old man was shaking so violently that his bed was moving slowly across the floor.

We laid our hands on him and rebuked the fever in the same way

Jesus did with Simon's wife's mother. How I wish I could tell you that the results were equally dramatic. They were not. However, the old man did recover in a few days and all was well.

I often wonder to myself if, when the apostle Paul used the medical *sunecho* when he said 'the love of Christ constrains us', he had in mind the idea that Christ's love has the same impact upon us, if we let it, as a raging fever. Certainly it was so with the apostle Paul. He had never forgotten, I am sure, the day when he knelt in the dust of the Damascus road and the germ of God's love had got into his spiritual bloodstream pushing up his spiritual temperature and setting fire to his soul. From that moment to the time of his death, everywhere he went he was like a man burning up with a raging fever – the fever of divine love.

Just look at the life of the apostle after he met with Christ on the Damascus road. Someone has said 'tracing the journeys of the apostle Paul across the ancient world is like tracing the track of a bleeding hare across the snow'. Wherever he went he met with opposition, sometimes having his blood shed in the course of preaching the gospel, yet his passion for spreading the message of Christ's love never once seems to have dimmed.

No sooner has he established one church than he is off into what he called 'the regions beyond'. It is impossible to account for the passion that burned in the heart of the great apostle Paul apart from the love of Christ.

Permit me to ask you this personal question: What drives you? What makes you tick? If your life could be stripped down right here and now to its irreducible minimum what is the motivating force that drives you forward in your Christian pilgrimage?

Sometimes I look back to the early years of my ministry and my heart is ashamed. So much of what I did was motivated by the itch to prove that I could do it, the covert bid for attention, the deep desire for approval. I was several years into my ministry before I realised I was more taken up with the cause of Christ rather than with Christ Himself. That realisation resulted in a fresh vision and a new anointing moving upon my life.

One of the saddest things to behold, in my opinion, is a Christian who is content with practising the duties of the Christian life and relying on them to bring satisfaction to the soul rather than a dynamic and passionate relationship with God. Our souls are capable of great passion – we see this in great music and great art.

Clearly when we look into the pages of the New Testament we see that the apostle Paul was a man who was burning up with the fever of God's love. *The love of Christ was the secret of his spiritual drive.*

Look now at the second passage, Luke 8:42–48:

As Jesus was on his way, the crowds almost crushed him. And a woman was there who had been subject to bleeding for twelve years, but no-one could heal her. She came up behind him and touched the edge of his cloak, and immediately her bleeding stopped.

'Who touched me?' Jesus asked.

When they all denied it, Peter said, 'Master, the people are crowding and pressing against you.'

But Jesus said, 'Someone touched me; I know that power has gone out from me.'

Then the woman, seeing that she could not go unnoticed, came trembling and fell at his feet. In the presence of all the people, she told why she had touched him and how she had been instantly healed. Then he said to her, 'Daughter, your faith has healed you. Go in peace.'

Jesus is passing through a certain place when crowds of people gather around Him and press Him on every side. Throughout His public ministry ordinary men and women flocked to hear the words that fell from the lips of our Lord and witness His astonishing miracles. When He spoke, the storms in men and women's hearts were hushed; His healing power set them free from their physical infirmities. Is it any wonder that wherever He went crowds of people surrounded Him?

Suddenly, a woman who had a longstanding physical problem, sees a gap in the crowd and rushes forward to touch the edge of Christ's garments. Instantly her bleeding stops and she is made perfectly whole.

Jesus turns and asks, 'Who touched me?' No one is willing to admit touching Him and when the disciples point out that the crowd are pressing upon Him in all directions, the Master replies, 'Someone touched me; I know that power has gone out of me.' At that point the woman who had touched Him confessed that she had been the one and our Lord's response to this was to congratulate her on the quality of her faith.

Note again the words of the disciples: '*the people are crowding and pressing against you ...*' The words 'crowding' and 'pressing' are taken again from the word *sunecho*. This too could justifiably be translated the people *constrain* You, they are all around You ... pressing upon You from every side.

Clearly the Gospel writer Luke is using the word *sunecho* here in the sense of our Lord being encircled and surrounded by a multitude of people. People were pressing in upon Him from every side, in front, behind and on both sides. Perhaps this might have been the thought that Paul had in mind when he talked about the love of Christ constraining us.

More than almost any other New Testament writer (perhaps with the exception of the apostle John), Paul seemed to revel in the fact that his life was circumscribed by the love of God. He saw it as encircling his life like a giant tourniquet holding him spiritually safe and secure in the midst of all life's problems. And the apostle seemed to have to face an endless array of problems. Someone has said of him that 'he was brought up in the university of adversity where the school colours were black and blue.'

But listen to what he says in Romans 8:35–39:

Who shall separate us from the love of Christ? Shall trouble or hardship or persecution or famine or nakedness or danger or sword? As it is written:

'For your sake we face death all day long;
   we are considered as sheep to be slaughtered.'

No, in all these things we are more than conquerors through him who loved us. For I am convinced that neither death nor life, neither angels nor demons, neither the present nor the future, nor any powers, neither height nor depth, nor anything else in all creation, will be able to separate us from the love of God that is in Christ Jesus our Lord.

Paul was convinced that everything that happened to him had first to pass the protective walls of God's love that encircled him and unless it furthered God's purposes in his life it would not be permitted to happen. When writing to the Philippians he said, 'Now I want you to know, brothers, that what has happened to me has really served to advance the gospel. As a result, it has become clear throughout the whole palace guard and to everyone else that I am in chains for Christ. Because of my chains, most of the brothers in the Lord have been encouraged to speak the word of God more courageously and fearlessly' (Phil. 1:12–14).

Often during an interview I have been asked, 'What's the greatest insight you have ever received from your study of the Scriptures?' I usually reply that the greatest insight that has ever come to me through the Scriptures is that the blood of Jesus Christ God's Son cleanses from all sin! And then I go on to say, 'If you want to know the second it is this: so encompassing is the love of God that nothing can ever get through it unless God foresees that He can work it for good in a Christian's life.'

One song writer put it like this:

Not one shaft can hit
Till his love sees fit.

This gripping truth ought to make us irrepressible. It certainly seems to have done that for the apostle Paul. His writings are punctuated with statements such as this: 'But thanks be to God! He gives us the victory through our Lord Jesus Christ' (1 Cor. 15:57). And this: 'In all these things we are more than conquerors through him who loved us' (Rom. 8:37). Clearly the love of Christ was not only the secret of his spiritual drive, *it was also the secret of his spiritual defence.*

Look now at the third passage, this time found in Luke 12:49–53:

'I have come to bring fire on the earth, and how I wish it were already kindled! But I have a baptism to undergo, and how distressed I am until it is completed! Do you think I came to bring peace on earth? No, I tell you, but division. From now on there will be five in one family divided against each other, three against two and two against three. They will be divided, father against son and son against father, mother against daughter and daughter against mother, mother-in-law against daughter-in-law and daughter in law against mother in law.

Our Lord here is reflecting on His ministry – a ministry that inevitably caused and created division. Christ demanded of His disciples that He be first and foremost in everything – before mother, father, brother, sister ... and so on. He knew this would not sit well with families who expected their loved ones to put them first in their affections. But Christ could not build His kingdom with disciples who had split allegiances. His instructions must be complied with to the letter or else, as He put it in Luke 14:26, 'you cannot be my disciples'.

Jesus, being a man of peace, knew this conflict would inevitably arise in families and, in uttering the words 'how distressed I am until it is completed', He is clearly looking forward to the cross and wishing the hour of His final suffering was already past. The word 'distressed' here, once again, is translated from the Greek word *sunecho*. The Amplified Bible translates it in this way: 'I have a baptism with which to be baptized, and how greatly and sorely I am urged on (impelled, constrained) until it is accomplished'. Eugene Peterson in *The Message* helpfully puts it like this: 'I've come to change everything, turn everything right side up – how I long for it to be finished'.

When I once asked a medical doctor friend of mine what he thought Jesus was feeling here, he said it was a sense of heaviness in His diaphragm brought about by His eagerness to complete the task He had been given by his Father. 'It is the kind of feeling one gets', he said, 'on the eve of an examination. You have prepared and now you just can't wait to get to grips with it'.

Perhaps that might also have been the thought in Paul's mind when he wrote to the Corinthians – the love of Christ *constrains* us – the passionate longing to complete the task given him by God. The great apostle had been given a work to do for God and he would allow nothing to hinder him until it was finished. No sooner had he evangelised one area and established there a New Testament church than he was on to those 'regions beyond'.

A friend of mine who is a Greek scholar suggests that the word *sunecho* as used in the passage could well be translated *desperate*. 'How I am made desperate until it be accomplished.' We just need to be a little careful, however, when using the word desperate as it can be used in two senses: desperate because one does not know what to do, or desperate in the sense of wanting to come to grips with important and urgent matters. Clearly the latter is the sense in which Jesus was using the word and so it would be also for the apostle Paul.

The theologian Karl Barth said somewhere in his writings that the word that came to mind when he looked at the life of the apostle Paul was also the word 'desperate'. I don't wonder. There seemed to be a holy desperation about him as he moved across the ancient world planting one church after another and never flagging in his zeal to proclaim Christ to everyone he met. He knew where he was going, what he had to do for God and would allow nothing to deter him until was it accomplished. *The love of Christ was the secret of his spiritual desperation.*

I wonder can the same be said of you? Are you a desperate man? Are you a desperate woman? Does the urgency of sharing the gospel with a world that is lost and bound for hell cause you to check up on your life from time to time and plead with God to show you what else you might to do help win men and women to Jesus Christ?

Let me turn once again to the question I asked at the commencement of this message: What drives you? What makes you tick? If your life could be stripped down right here and now to its irreducible minimum what is the motivating force that drives you forward in your Christian pilgrimage?

I trust that, like Paul for whom the love of Christ was the secret of his spiritual drive, his spiritual defence and his spiritual desperation, it might be the same for every one of us.

It is certainly my deepest spiritual longing.

I hope it is yours also.

7

THE FOUR MARKS OF A HEALTHY PERSONALITY

JOHN 13:1–11

Jesus knew that the Father had put all things under his power, and that he had come from God and was returning to God; so he got up from the meal, took off his outer clothing, and wrapped a towel round his waist. After that, he poured water into a basin and began to wash his disciples' feet, drying them with the towel that was wrapped round him. (vv.3–5)

Several years ago, on one of my visits to the United States, I was given a tape recording of a valedictory service held at Harvard University. Over a hundred students who had been trained in psychiatry were about to graduate and before being given their graduation credentials one of the professors gave an address which was not only appropriate to the occasion but was filled with some of the most wonderful and interesting insights I have ever heard.

He identified for the graduates what he called the 'four marks of a healthy personality', his point being that only as they understood these characteristics and made them integral to their lives could they model them to others.

A healthy personality, he said, will have at least four elements:

A clear sense of identity and being comfortable with that;
A loving spirit that reaches out to others;
A sensitive conscience that knows right from wrong;
A healthy attitude towards one's death.

As I listened to him expand on those four elements there came singing into my consciousness the passage we have just read from John 13. It came home to me in a powerful way that Jesus exemplified every one of them in His life here on earth – and to the most perfect degree.

I would like now to focus on each of these four points to see not only how they are so wonderfully exemplified in Christ, but also that they might become integral to our own lives.

1. A CLEAR SENSE OF IDENTITY AND BEING COMFORTABLE WITH THAT

One of the issues talked about a good deal in contemporary society is that of personal identity. The phrase 'identity crisis' is an expression that has formed part of our vocabulary for decades. By far the most questions asked of counsellors nowadays have to do with the issue of identity. People want help in finding out who they are and what they are doing here in the world – how they can discover what is called 'the authentic self'.

But what do we mean when we talk about identity? One dictionary of psychology defines it in this way: *the ability of a person to give a clear and concise answer to the question: who am I?* When it comes to the issue of what *constitutes* identity I have always liked the explanation of Dr Clyde Narramore of The Rosemead Graduate School of Psychology, California at whose college I trained as a counsellor.

He says that we need three things in order to construct a strong sense of identity. First, a *sense of belonging and of being unconditionally loved.* Second, a *high sense of self-worth,* and third, a *sense of meaning and purpose.* These three things he says are like a tripod on which we stand and if only one of those legs are shaky then our understanding of who we are will be shot through with insecurity.

Take the first – a sense of belonging and of being unconditionally loved. There is something warm and wonderful about knowing you belong to someone who loves you, and loves you unconditionally. For example, whenever I focus on the fact that I belong to the Creator and Redeemer of the universe and that I am the recipient of a love that will never be taken away, something powerful and profound moves within me. Someone has said: We don't know who we are until we know whose we are; the more aware I am that I am a child of the living God the more I find I am able to rise above my fears, deal with life on a more positive basis and give up my grudges more easily. If this first leg of the tripod is not firmly in place then there is little hope of establishing a strong sense of identity.

Take the second – a sense of self-worth. By this I mean a clear awareness of one's personal value. I believe every one of us has a need to feel valued in the eyes of at least one person. The 'self' really is a series of reflected appraisals. We value ourselves as we have been valued. Someone has put it like this: 'I am not what I think I am, I am not what you think I am, I am what I think you think I am.' The actual compass by which we steer is not what others think of us but what we think they think of us. Sadly, there are multitudes of people who have been deprived of loving relationships in their childhood and when they think of how others think of them, their hearts are filled with a variety of negative feelings. Such people, if they do not have a relationship with the God who created them are left with, to use Dr Clyde Narramore's metaphor, a very shaky leg to their tripod.

Consider now the third element which forms our personal identity – a sense of meaning and purpose. Just as everyone needs to feel that they belong and are unconditionally loved and have a strong sense of worth, so also do they need to feel there is a purpose to them being here on Planet Earth. And when that purpose has an eternal perspective to it – a purpose that continues beyond this life – then the meaning drawn from that enables people to deal with anything that life may throw at them.

No one who ever walked this earth was more clear about His identity than our Lord. Picture the scene with me that is presented by the passage before us. Our Lord is closeted with His disciples in the Upper Room. He is getting close to the hour of His death. Inside, the atmosphere is heavy with unborn events. Outside, a storm is about to be unleashed. But look at Jesus. How secure He seems. He takes bread and wine and shares it with His disciples. Facing an ignominious death on a cross, there is no hint of an identity crisis in Him.

John gives us a clue as to our Lord's security in these moments when he says: '*Jesus, knowing that the Father had given all things into his hands, and that he had come from God and was going to God ...*' (NKJV) The Saviour knew where He had come from and knew where He was going. John is painting an eternal perspective here. Christ came out of eternity and was now going back to it. I am convinced that the more our identity is rooted in an eternal perspective, as opposed to a temporal one, the more secure we will feel as persons.

I think Charles Wesley, the great hymn writer of a past century, clearly understood this great truth. It is said that in all he wrote about 7,000 hymns and of these a goodly number were composed to mark the major happenings in his own life. Among such occasional pieces one of the best known and best loved is the great hymn written on one of his birthdays which begins:

Away with our fears the glad morning appears
   When an heir of salvation was born
From Jehovah I came, for His glory I am
   And to Him I with singing return.

From Jehovah I came? What does he mean? Where does his father Samuel come in? And his heroic mother, Susannah?

Has he forgotten them? Oh, he is not at all unmindful of them but as he glances back across the years it is not of them he is thinking. His eyes see far beyond them. He is not celebrating his human parentage; he is singing his genealogy as a child of God!

Our identity must be rooted in something more than the temporal if it is to be complete. The statement I am now about to make will sound arrogant to an unbeliever but I am nevertheless certain it is true: only a person who has a personal relationship with Jesus Christ can have a clear and complete sense of identity. And why? Because only a Christian has an eternal perspective in which to operate. We too must sing our genealogy realising that we were predestinated in Christ before the foundation of the world and are destined to spend the whole of eternity with Him. Our Lord had a clear sense of His identity and, if we are to live effectively in this world, so must we also.

2. A LOVING SPIRIT THAT REACHES OUT TO OTHERS

We talked earlier about the importance of being unconditionally loved. Life, however, is not just about being the passive recipient of love but also about being the active dispenser of it. St Augustine in the fourth century said that before he found Christ he searched for something and someone to love and found himself, as he put it, in love with loving.

We should not be surprised that love plays such an important part in human life for we are built to love. Every single person on earth has been created in the image of the Trinity whose nature is love – love of the highest quality and in the highest degree possible.

Many years ago I came across a statement by the late D. Broughton Knox in which he attempted to explain the nature of the Trinity. It is one of the most profound and revealing statements concerning the Trinity I have ever read and one that has changed my outlook on the Godhead ever since.

> The Father loves the Son and gives Him everything. The Son always does that which pleases the Father. The Spirit takes of the things of the Son and shows them to us. He does not glorify Himself. We learn from the Trinity that relationship is the essence of reality and therefore the essence of our existence, and we also learn that the way this relationship should be expressed is by concern for others. Within the Trinity itself there is a concern by the persons of the Trinity for one another.[1]

Focus with me on that last sentence for a moment: *Within the Trinity itself there is a concern by the persons of the Trinity for one another.* Can you see what he is saying? The energy that pulses in the heart of the Trinity is other-centred. We who were designed by the Trinity are made to function in the same way. That is why self-centredness – the opposite of other-centredness – is the world's greatest insanity. I am convinced that if you could take self-centredness out of every human heart there would be very little personal problems left in the world.

John Stott has said: 'That self-centredness is a world-wide phenomenon is evident from the rich variety of words in our language which are compounded with "self"'. There are more than 50 that have a pejorative meaning – words like self-applause, self-absorption, self-assertion, self-advertisement, self-indulgence, self-gratification, self-glorification, self-pity, self-importance, self-interest and self-will.

Malcolm Muggeridge, the famous broadcaster and writer who became a Christian late in life used to talk about the 'dark little dungeon of the ego'. And what a dark dungeon it is. To be taken up with our own concerns and have no concern for the needs of others is to be confined and cramped in the most unhealthy of prisons.

When we fail to follow the design built into us by the Trinity – to be more concerned about others than we are about ourselves – then we are demeaned as persons. There is an amazing verse in Proverbs, that says, he who laughs at another's distress shall not go unpunished (17:5). What this text is saying is that unless we move with love towards those who are in distress then as sure as night follows day a toll will be taken in our inner being.

What is the punishment that is spoken of here? Does God come down and put some sickness on us or cause us to have an accident? No, the punishment is that something will die within us, our creativity will dry up, our zest for life will be eroded and our ability to withstand stress will be reduced. We cannot rise to the potential that God has built into us when we fail to love.

Look at how a loving spirit manifested itself in Jesus. On the eve of His death by crucifixion He took time to encourage and minister to His disciples. John tells us: '... having loved his own ... he loved them to the end' (John 13:1, NKJV). He kept on loving them despite their dullness, their blindness and their blundering ways. His was a loving spirit that reaches out to others and that spirit must possess us too.

3. A SENSITIVE CONSCIENCE THAT KNOWS RIGHT FROM WRONG
I must confess that as I listened to the professor making this third point, I considered it rather brave of him in the light of the postmodern culture which we find in most of our universities. Even the most casual observer of human affairs cannot help but notice that over the past few decades the distinctions between right and wrong generally speaking

are becoming clouded and blurred.

We are witnessing in our generation the most rapid cultural change since the Enlightenment. I strongly believe that future sociologists will look back at these past few decades and see them as one of the most critical turning points in history. When I came into the ministry in the early fifties I could take it for granted that people would know what I meant when I talked about God, the Bible, the Ten Commandments, right and wrong. They saw God as the Creator, a Judge, Lawgiver, the Sustainer of the Universe, Sovereign. They knew the Ten Commandments were a standard of morality, and most people had no difficulty in determining what was right and what was wrong. People were guided by Christian paradigms. But not anymore.

A recent TV programme on the subject of the Ten Commandments ended up by someone saying, 'Maybe we need another ten commandments, that accommodate themselves to the age in which we live.' Nothing sharpens the truth that there is a right and a wrong way to live like the Ten Commandments.

Charles Colson, who was President Nixon's right hand man and was converted shortly before being sent to prison, tells how he gave a talk to the students of Yale University in the USA on the subject of how Yale had contributed to undermining the rule of law, by separating morality from it.

He had tea with one of the lecturers who had invited him to give a talk and Colson said: 'I'm just a little concerned that what I will say might cause a riot.'

He was there to oppose the idea that Law has nothing to do with morality.

'No,' said his friend, 'let me tell you how it is nowadays. These students have been taught long before they got here that truth is relative. There is no objective truth any more. They won't even bother to argue; they will just shrug their shoulders and say "Well that's the truth as he sees it ... we see it differently." They will listen politely, take a few notes, pack up their papers and slip out into the night!

And that of course was exactly what they did.

Notice now how Jesus dealt with this issue of right and wrong. In another Gospel – the Gospel of Luke – it is clear that around this time (Luke 22) there was an argument going on amongst the disciples as to who would be the greatest in the kingdom of God. How does Jesus deal with this wrong attitude amongst the disciples? Does He rebuke them and remonstrate with them? As other parts of the Gospel show, He was not above giving rebuke, but in this instance He deals with the situation differently.

The account in John's Gospel says:

Jesus knew that the Father had put all things under his power, and that he had come from God and was returning to God; so he got up from the meal, took off his outer clothing, and wrapped a towel around his waist. After that, he poured water into a basin and began to wash his disciples' feet, drying them with the towel that was wrapped around him.

Jesus was always adept and creative at bringing issues to a head. Knowing that sometimes we are more affected by something we see than something we hear, our Lord adopts the position of a servant, takes a towel and a bowl of water and begins to wash their feet. In the magnificent eloquence of a deed He stood up for what was right even though it meant Him getting down on His knees! The Master intended to show His bickering disciples that humility is the hallmark of everything spiritual.

In a little while Jesus would have to confront a cross but first He confronted a towel. A great Welsh preacher, Dr Cynddylan Jones, once said, 'Some might find it easier to confront a cross than a towel; the cross demands courage, but the towel – humility. It is humility that presents us with one of life's greatest challenges.'

It is another strong conviction of mine that we cannot arrive at a healthy condition in our souls unless we have a sensitive conscience that knows the difference between right and wrong. And not only to know the difference but to confront things that are wrong in a spirit of humility, not by preaching thundering sermons at people.

How do we gain a sensitive conscience that knows the difference between right and wrong? By staying close to Christ and following the truths He has laid down for us in the Scriptures.

4. A HEALTHY ATTITUDE TOWARDS ONE'S DEATH

Almost everyone has a fear of death. It has been said that this fear is as *old* as human life, as *long* as human life and as *widespread* as human life.

Some people are quite unwilling to face it. They thrust it from their own thoughts and the mention of it by others is considered by them to be 'morbid'. Death for some people is one of the greatest anxiety provokers that there is.

The fact of death however must be faced for at some time in the future everyone listening to me will die. As George Bernard Shaw said: 'The statistics concerning death are very impressive!' An unwillingness to face the fact of one's finitude is unhealthy and detrimental to good psychological and spiritual health.

I have often wondered when I will die, where I will die, how I will die. I do not reflect on this in a morbid way but rather out of curiosity. Many know I have an incurable cancer (incurable in human terms) and I have long ago moved into NTBR bracket (not to be resuscitated) when some young, wise and clever white-coated doctor will look me over and decide in his wisdom that I am not worth keeping alive. So for me death is not that far distant. Heaven is becoming more of a reality to me than earth.

Jesus, when He was here on earth, did not say a great deal about heaven but what He did say was very significant. 'In my Father's house,' He said, 'are many rooms; if it were not so, I would have told you.' What did He call heaven? *My Father's house!* Though in the frailty of my nature I carry a concern about the manner of my dying I set against that the glorious fact that death has one mission – to conduct me into my Father's more immediate presence and give me an abiding place in the great company of the redeemed.

How did Jesus see death? Listen once more to the account: 'Jesus knew that the Father had put all things under his power, and that he had come from God and was *returning to God* ...' He saw death as going to God.

In parts of Africa Christians, when talking of fellow believers who have died, do not refer to them as 'gone' but as having 'arrived'. Many years ago an army officer by the name of Colonel David Marcus was killed in action. Before he was buried the contents of his pockets were put together and sent to his widow. She was greatly comforted by one thing that he was carrying when he died. It was a little bit of paper entitled 'The Ship'. She didn't know where the Colonel had got it but it meant much to her:

I am standing upon the sea-shore. A ship at my side spreads her white sails in the morning breeze and starts for the blue ocean. She is an object of beauty and strength and I stand and watch her until at length she is only a ribbon of white cloud just where the sea and the sky come to mingle with each other. Then someone at my side says 'There! She's gone!'

Gone where? Gone from my sight – that is all. She is just as large in mast and hull and spar as she was when she left my side and just as able to bear her load of living freight to the place of her destination. Her diminished size is in me, not in her and just as the moment when someone at my side says 'There! She's gone!' there are other voices ready to take up the glad shout, 'There! She comes!'

And that, for a Christian is dying!

Let me in these closing moments turn your gaze once more on Jesus. He is so wonderful isn't He? Never did human form hold one so adorable. He is the model of how we should live and all that we seek to do in this world. In Him we see the marks of a full and glorious humanity.

Our heart's cry should constantly be: How can we be more like Him? For the more we become like Him the more impact we will make on the lives of those we touch day by day. Then we will be able to say with full meaning: For me to live is Christ and to die ...

To die?

To die, my dear friends, in Jesus.

To die ... is GAIN.

NOTE

1. D. Broughton Knox, *The Everlasting God* (Evangelical Press, 1982).

~8~
THE CHALLENGE
TO LOVE AGAIN

JOHN 21:15–18

When they had finished eating, Jesus said to Simon Peter, 'Simon son of John, do you truly love me more than these?'

'Yes, Lord,' he said, 'you know that I love you.'

Jesus said, 'Feed my lambs.'

Again Jesus said, 'Simon son of John, do you truly love me?'

He answered, 'Yes, Lord, you know that I love you.'

Jesus said, 'Take care of my sheep.'

The third time he said to him, 'Simon son of John, do you love me?'

Peter was hurt because Jesus asked him the third time, 'Do you love me?' He said, 'Lord, you know all things; you know that I love you.'

Jesus said, 'Feed my sheep. I tell you the truth, when you were younger you dressed yourself and went where you wanted; but when you are old you will stretch out your hands, and someone else will dress you and lead you where you do not want to go.' Jesus said this to indicate the kind of death by which Peter would glorify God. Then he said to him, 'Follow me!'

~

One of the last things Jesus Christ did before He left this world was to confront Simon Peter with one of the most piercing and personal questions that anyone can ask of another. What was it? Peter, have you mastered the technical details of My religion? No. Peter, have you grasped the great scheme of God in allowing Me to die and be raised again? No, not even that. Peter do you know how to raise funds for the continuation of My ministry? No.

The question as we have seen in the passage before us was this: *Peter, do you love me?* In fact our Lord put that question to Peter three times. What was the point of this thrice-repeated question? I believe the answer to be that it took Peter to the central issue of the spiritual life – how deep was his love for Jesus?

When Christianity is brought down to its irreducible minimum it is not about how orthodox is our doctrine or how efficient is our service; or even how blameless is our character. Not that these things are unimportant but they are not the central issue. The central issue of the Christian life, I say again, is how deep is our love for Jesus. This really is the core of Christianity.

Our Lord had given Simon Peter a great deal of personal attention because He knew that one day in the not too distant future the affairs of the kingdom would be largely placed in his hands. To him would be given on the Day of Pentecost the 'keys of the kingdom' and it would be his privilege to be the first to open the door of that kingdom to 3,000 new-born souls.

Perhaps it was because our Lord knew the significant role Simon Peter would play in the formation of the Church that He singled him out from amongst the other disciples and put to him that thrice-repeated question. This was the Saviour's last opportunity to prepare the vacillating Simon for the work that lay ahead.

Before we look more deeply at the point and purpose of our Lord's question permit me, by way of preamble, to focus on a few important considerations. I have come to believe that our biggest failures in the Christian life are those connected with our inability to love. That certainly is where I fail the most and if my experience is anything to go by in talking to Christians down the years, it seems to be the failure of many other believers also.

You will be aware I am sure that when it comes to defining love there are endless definitions to be found in both secular and Christian literature. Charles Finney, the great revivalist of a past generation, said, 'Love is bringing about the highest good in the life of another person.' In the film *Love Story*, love is defined as 'never having to say you are sorry.' (That definition is too idealistic to be real, in my opinion.)

A definition of love that has come to have great meaning for me is that given by my friend Dr Larry Crabb, a psychologist who lives in the USA. 'Love,' he said, 'is moving toward others without self-protection.' It is a narrow definition of course and really deals with just one aspect of love, but I want to pick up that definition and consider it in more detail before we apply it to the conversation between Jesus and Simon Peter in the passage we have just read.

Suppose you are in a relationship with someone and you know that in their own interests and the interests of the kingdom you have to lovingly confront them over an issue which might cause them to reject you. No one likes being rejected and you can protect yourself from the pain of rejection by simply avoiding the confrontation. Instead of moving towards them and risking getting rejected or rebuffed you can go in the opposite direction and thus avoid the hurt. But now what have you done? Your choice to be self-protective and not to confront has meant there has been a failure in love.

A failure in love takes place when we are governed more by fear than by love; when we are more concerned about our own emotional protection than in doing the loving thing. There are two great forces that govern our lives – love and fear. When love flows in, fear flows out. When fear flows in, love flows out. It is as simple as that. The more love fills our heart the less fear can take a hold. Scripture puts it succinctly when it says, '... perfect love drives out fear' (1 John 4:18).

An old secular song says, 'love is the reason for living'. Another way of saying it is that love is the purpose of living. A quick look at an incident in the life of Jesus might help us see the relevance and importance of this. One day a teacher of the Law asked this question of the Saviour: 'Of all the commandments, which is the most important?' (Mark 12:28).

At that moment I can visualise in my mind the angels leaning over the battlements of heaven and wondering to themselves which of the Ten Commandments Jesus would choose. Our Lord replied, 'The most important one is this: "Hear, O Israel, the Lord our God, the Lord is one. Love the Lord your God with all your heart and with all your soul and with all your mind and with all your strength." The second is this: "Love your neighbour as yourself." There is no commandment greater than these' (vv.29–31).

The two that Christ chose, loving God and loving one's neighbour as oneself, summarise of course the whole of the Ten Commandments. However, in another place (John 13:34) Jesus talks about another commandment: 'A new commandment I give to you, that you love one another; as I have loved you ...' (NKJV). So are there now eleven commandments and not just ten? No, this new commandment about which Jesus speaks simply introduces a new dimension into the concept of love. From that moment on the true measurement of love is to love in the same way Jesus loved.

As I have loved you. Note that.

And how does Christ love? Fully, perfectly and without self-protection. How many times did the disciples hurt Him by their obstinacies, their dullness and disloyalties, their unwillingness to stay in the path He marked out for them, but He still came to them with love in His eyes, willing to be hurt again and again because His love had no failure in it. It was said of Him in John 13:1: 'Having loved His own ... He loved them to the end (NKJV).

Having looked at the example of Christ's love and having considered His words in John 13 we are now in a better position to see that the purpose of living is this – *to love as we are loved!* When it comes down to it this is what life is all about: *loving involvement with God and loving involvement with others.* And it is here, I say again, where we fail the most. It was Simon Peter's biggest failure, it is my biggest failure and if you look carefully into your own heart I am sure you will agree it is yours also.

Loving involvement with God of course carries no problems, but what about loving involvement with others? 'Ah,' as Shakespeare said, 'there's the rub'! Even Christians can be difficult to relate to sometimes. A friend of mine, a pastor, warns young converts that when they mix with other Christians not to be too surprised if they feel let down or disappointed. 'Christians.' he says, 'are not angels, and your task is to keep your eyes on Jesus. Live closely to Him and be an example to those who perhaps are much younger than you in the faith.' Wise advice.

A story is told of a janitor in a Scottish church who was picking up bits of paper after a Sunday morning service and came across a rhyme that no doubt was the result of someone's doodling:

> To dwell above with saints we love,
>   My that will be glory
> To dwell below with saints we know,
>   Now that's a different story.

Those involved in Christian ministry discover all too often that God calls us to move towards people who are guaranteed to hurt us. So what can we do to avoid such hurts? We can arrange our relationships in such a way that we get close enough to people to be affirmed by them but not close enough to be hurt by them. But then that is a failure in love.

In effect we are saying to God: I am not sure that your resources are strong enough to hold me in this situation so I will protect myself from any possible hurt through superficial relationships. And let's face it – that basically is a lack of trust. It is tantamount to saying to the Almighty: I have more confidence in my ability to protect myself than in Your ability to hold me securely in the face of possible hurt.

Against this background let's take a closer look at this loveable but blundering disciple we know as Simon Peter. It seems that almost every time he opened his mouth he put his foot in it. Someone said, when you get to heaven if you want to find Simon Peter look for someone with a foot-shaped mouth!

Consider just three of his blunderings – there are many more. He blundered when he tried to divert Christ from going to the cross (Matt. 16:22). He blundered again on the Mount of Transfiguration when he tried to persuade Christ to remain there, offering to build three shelters, one for Moses, one for Elijah and one for Christ (Matt. 17:4). He blundered a third time when Jesus told him, "'I tell you the truth, this very night, before the cock crows, you will disown me three times.' But Peter declared, "Even if I have to die with you, I will never disown you'" (Matt. 26:34–35).

But he did.

What caused Simon Peter to deny his relationship with Christ three times as he warmed himself at the charcoal fire? Probably he was disillusioned with the way things had gone. Jesus had presented Himself to the disciples as the Messiah and part of the Messiah's mission was to restore the kingdom of Israel. But now Jesus was in captivity and all the hopes Peter had invested in Him appeared to be shattered. It is so easy when we are disillusioned to make decisions that cause a lifetime of regret.

While Peter warms himself at the fire Jesus, escorted by soldiers, passes by on the way to His trial and looks at him. There was something about that look that went deep into the soul of Simon Peter causing him to weep bitterly. A sense of disloyalty and regret sweeps over him like a flood and he shakes with sobs.

I have often wondered what it was about that look Jesus gave Simon Peter that caused him to weep such copious tears. What did it say? Only Peter of course could have known what those eyes were saying to him but many painters and artists have tried to capture it. I have lingered in many an art gallery over the years studying paintings of artists who felt they interpreted the look that Jesus gave Simon Peter that day, but none of them in my view captured what I consider was the true expression on our Lord's face.

So what kind of look was it? A look of scorn? I think not. Disappointment? No. Derision? Most certainly not that. Rebuke? No, not that either. Anger or indignation?

Again no.

Hurt? Perhaps. Yes, hours of thinking on this issue convince me it could have been hurt. But there was something else going on in our Lord that needs to be understood. Perhaps an explanation of how our emotions work might help you see the point I am making here. I do not believe that anger is always a *primary* emotion. Often before we feel anger we feel hurt and because we don't like the feelings that come from hurt we overlay it with anger. Anger is a more delicious feeling than hurt!

I believe that when Jesus looked at Simon Peter there would have been a look of hurt without any overlay of anger or rejection in it. It was that, I believe, which broke him, a tender wounded look that unsealed the fountain of tears.

Listen carefully to this next sentence: *When you gaze upon the face of someone you have hurt and you see hurt but no rejection in that look you have just had a glimpse of the face of Jesus Christ!*

Consider now what happens to Simon Peter after the moment when he went out and wept bitterly. He was nowhere to be seen at the time of crucifixion and though he appears again after the resurrection he returns in due course to his fishing nets on the lake of Galilee. That's where we catch up with him in the passage we read earlier – John 21.

Peter was not able to love well so he goes back to doing what he knows how to do well – catch fish. It's interesting when we can't love well we fall back to doing other things we know we can do well. When I don't feel like loving well I write about it, or preach about it.

Perhaps you may be wondering what I mean by 'loving well'? Loving well is when, though our own hearts may be hurting and we may be in the deepest pain, we can still move towards others without self-protection. It may not be easy but it is always possible. Never forget that. Our Lord not only lifts the standards to almost unbelievable heights but He also provides the power by which we reach up to them.

Often we refuse to rise above our own pain and reach out to heal the pain of others believing that our pain exempts us and excuses us from loving well. At such times we are far from being the kind of disciples that Christ is looking for.

When we meet up with Simon Peter and some of the other disciples in John 21 we find them having had an unsuccessful night of fishing. They had caught nothing. As the dawn breaks over Galilee the disciples hear a voice from the shore asking: 'Have you any fish?'

'No,' they respond.

'Then throw your net on the right side of the ship,' says the stranger on the shore. Perhaps figuring that the person standing on the shore could see something they couldn't, they obey and immediately all the fish that had been avoiding their net throughout the night began swimming into it.

Here they come one after the other – 10, 20, 30, 40, 50, 60, 70, 80, 90, 100 ... until finally there are 153 fish in the net! At this point Simon Peter realises that what they were witnessing was a miracle and, connecting it to Christ, he jumps into the water and makes for the shore. The other disciples followed in the boat, towing the net full of fish. When they landed they saw a fire of burning coals there with fish on it, and some bread.

Jesus invites them to bring some of the fish they had caught and as they sit together eating breakfast he turns to Simon Peter and says, 'Simon son of John, do you truly love me more than these?' The question needs the beckoning of the hand to truly understand it. Some commentators believe that Jesus pointed to the other disciples at that moment, while others believe He pointed to the fish.

In my judgment it makes more sense to accept that Jesus was pointing to the fish. It was fish after all that had played a strategic part in Simon Peter's life. It was a miraculous catch of fish, remember, that first caused Simon Peter to become a follower of the Master. Then there was the occasion when Peter approached the Master and asked Him if they should pay the tax to the Temple. Jesus told him to go down to the sea, catch the first fish he saw and said that he would find in its mouth enough money to pay the tax to the Temple for both of them.

Now here again on the Lake of Galilee Peter had witnessed another miracle concerning fish. Three times the Saviour had worked a miracle with fish in order to convince Simon Peter of His desire to be involved in his life. Did Peter remember at that moment I wonder that Jesus had called him away from the fishing nets to become a fisher of men? And where did he turn when it looked as if the enterprise which Jesus had started was about to fall apart? Back to the fish.

I think all this gives credence to the idea that when Jesus said, 'Do you love me more than these?' our Lord would have pointed in the direction of the miraculous catch of fish which He had just given to them. Peter's response to our Lord's question was 'Yes, Lord, you know that I love you.' Jesus said, 'Feed my lambs.'

Jesus then asked for the second time, 'Simon son of John, do you truly love me?' Peter answered, 'Yes, Lord, you know that I love you.' Jesus said, 'Take care of my sheep.'

Jesus then asked a third time, 'Simon son of John, do you love me?' Peter, we read, was hurt because the Lord asked him the same question the third time and he replied, 'Lord, you know all things; you know that I love you.' Jesus said, 'Feed my sheep.'

It is clear throughout this whole conversation that Peter is on the defensive in answering our Lord's question 'Do you love me?' He had, after all, proved by his failure that his love for Christ was not enduring. Now he was being asked if he was ready to love again, to make a new commitment to the Saviour whom he had denied. Still unsure of himself, no wonder he felt hurt at the Lord's gentle persistence. His distress is very apparent.

I think in order to understand the dynamics that were taking place in this spiritual tête à tête between Jesus and Simon Peter we can be helped greatly by reading the account in the J.B. Phillips translation. J.B. Phillips points out that two Greek words are being used in this conversation: agape and philia. He claims that the first time Jesus asked, 'Do you love me?' He used the robust Greek word agape. When Simon Peter replied he used the weaker Greek word, philia meaning friend.

To understand the deep import of what was happening here picture yourself asking someone whose love meant much to you, 'Do you love me?' and they respond by saying 'I like you. Perhaps you would be too hurt to risk making yourself vulnerable a second time and withdraw behind the layers of self-protection. There is after all hardly anything as hurtful and devastating as unreciprocated love.

The same happens the second time Jesus asks the question. He uses the strong Greek word *agape*. 'Do you love me?' Peter responds once again with the weaker word – *philia*. 'You know that I am your friend.'

But Jesus who 'loves without self-protection' continues to make Himself vulnerable.

The third time Jesus asks the question, however, He takes the word that Peter had been using (*philia*) off his lips and says, 'Simon, son of John, are you my friend?' It was as if our Lord was saying: 'Peter is this all I mean to you? Look, if it's fish you want, I can give you the biggest and the best catch you have ever known. Will you now consider what I want? I want your full allegiance. Peter, above all things I want your love.'

How wonderfully this story would have ended if Peter had come out from behind the weaker word (*philia*) and said, 'Yes Lord, I love (*agape*) you.' But he didn't. Once again he used the weaker word: 'Lord, you know everything, you know that I am your friend.'

It looks like another failure on Simon Peter's part doesn't it? But perhaps things might not be as they first appear. Previously Peter had promised a perfect commitment and failed. Maybe now he wasn't going to make the same mistake again. Perhaps something had been humbled within him. Failure might have made him less self-reliant and more ready for a more honest facing of himself. This might have been the strategy behind our Lord's question – to surface in Peter a deeper self-understanding and a more honest approach to the issues going on in his soul.

Whatever went on in Simon Peter's life between that moment and the Day of Pentecost we can only conjecture. Whatever it was I am sure the Master's last question to Peter brought him into a deeper understanding of himself and of his Lord and prepared him for his encounter with the Spirit on the Day of Pentecost. How comforting it is to know that in Christ we are dealing with Someone who when we hurt Him by our failures and our obstinacies nevertheless goes on loving still. We may fail Him but He never fails us.

I wonder, am I talking to someone now who might be in the very same place as Simon Peter? Something has disillusioned you in the Christian life. Perhaps God never answered a prayer in the way you thought He should. Maybe things have not turned out the way you expected and you feel hurt, and your love for the Lord no longer flows warm and free. Perhaps you have failed the Lord so many times you feel He would never want to have a relationship with you again.

Well, our Lord's dealings with Simon Peter show that is not true. And just as He probed the heart of Peter, maybe He is probing your heart at this moment. Because of our Lord's ability to love perfectly, to love unconditionally, to love without self-protection, the good news is it is possible to fail without losing our relationship with Him. No matter how much we fail He will come to us in our darkest and dreariest hour inviting us to open our hearts to Him once more, daring us to love again. And in the strength and knowledge of that, maybe we will fail less.

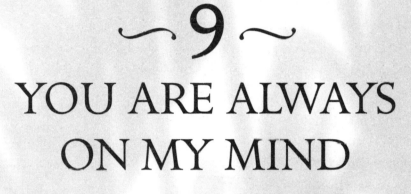

~9~

YOU ARE ALWAYS
ON MY MIND

PSALM 139

O LORD, you have searched me and you know me.
You know when I sit and when I rise;
  you perceive my thoughts from afar.
You discern my going out and my lying down;
  you are familiar with all my ways.
Before a word is on my tongue
  you know it completely, O LORD.
You hem me in – behind and before;
  you have laid your hand upon me.
Such knowledge is too wonderful for me,
  too lofty for me to attain. (vv.1–6)

Some time ago I found inside my Saturday morning newspaper a free CD entitled '40 Greatest Ever Love Songs'. I listened to them on my CD player and while some of them were not to my taste there was one that caught my interest. It was a song first made popular by Elvis Presley and now was being sung by Willie Nelson entitled 'You are always on my mind'.

It's a song about a man who didn't treat his wife in the way he should and one day he comes to see how foolish he had been. It's really a lament and apology for not seeing her true value and worth. Here's one of the verses:

Maybe I didn't hold you
All those lonely, lonely times
I guess I never told you,
I'm so happy that you're mine
Little things I should have said and done
I just never took the time
You are always on my mind
You are always on my mind.

As I listened to those words the words of the psalm we have just read floated into my mind. Clearly the main thrust of the 139th Psalm is simply this – *the Eternal God always has us on His mind.*

Some find it incredible that the God who created such a vast universe should take an interest in the affairs of such puny creatures here on earth, let alone keep us always in mind. And when you think about it, it is not difficult to understand why they come to that conclusion. They look out at this vast universe and listen to the astronomers who tell us that when they put their eye to the strongest telescopes they discover we are living in an expanding universe and however hard they try they cannot find the hem on the skirt of creation's garment. In the bewildering vastness of space it seems somewhat incongruous to even ask the question, Does the great Creator God *think* about me? Is He interested in what I do here on Planet Earth? Does He long to have fellowship with my poor heart? To some people set against this great and vast and measureless universe with its exhaustless profusion of suns, stars and systems, those questions seem pathetically irrelevant and unimportant.

So can we really believe that the Creator and Sustainer of the Universe notices the presence of separate persons on this microscopic earth? Does the God who built a universe that baffles the greatest scientific minds take a *Father's* interest in His children? The answer of the psalmist is of course – YES. He is far, far, above our thought, but on the authority of His Word we dare believe that His thoughts are ever towards us. Though whirling worlds move at His word, it is not the mountains, or the stars, or the galaxies He thinks most about, but you and me. This psalm confirms that exciting truth in a most wonderful way.

It begins with David declaring that God knows everything about him. 'You *have searched me and you know me*.' How did God know David? By researching him. We are all familiar with research projects. We do them at school and at work. We study something in order to know almost all there is to know about it. The Almighty has made every one of us His personal research project – He has researched every one of us and knows not *almost* everything there is to know about us, but every single thing – down to the tiniest detail.

> God researched David's lifestyle: *You know when I sit and when I rise*
>
> He researched his thoughts: *you perceive my thoughts from afar*
>
> He researched his public life: *You discern my going out …*
>
> He researched his private life: *… and my lying down*
>
> Summing it all up, he says: *you are familiar with all my ways*.

Then he adds this: '*Before a word is on my tongue you know it completely, O* LORD'. I have often been fascinated with the fact – and I am sure you have too – that people who have been married to each other for many years can often finish each other's sentences. But God doesn't have to finish our sentences, He knows what we are going to say before we say it!

The thought of an omniscient God is scary to some people. We worry about people knowing too much about us. We take all the steps we can to guard our privacy. In the modern world we have a new form of theft called 'identity theft'. It takes place when someone steals a person's credit card number, their pin number, their home address or their date of birth and fraudulently uses that information to their own advantage. However the fact that God knows everything about him does not appear to frighten the psalmist. But though he is not frightened, he certainly stands in awe of the fact: 'Such knowledge is too wonderful for me, too lofty for me to attain', he says.

Consider this also: God knows the worst about us so there is no discovery about any one of us that can disillusion Him, in the way we get disillusioned when we discover something in us we wish was not there. Isn't it a shock to the system when you realise that within you there is a sinful disposition that if you were to go along with is capable of doing the most horrible things? God knows our potential for evil better than we do but He allows nothing to quench His determination to bless us and minister to us. He is not against us for our sin but for us against our sin.

David goes on to say that God is tracking us every moment of our existence. Listen to this:

> Where can I go from your Spirit?
>   Where can I flee from your presence?
> If I go up to the heavens, you are there;
>   if I make my bed in the depths, you are there.
> If I rise on the wings of the dawn,
>   if I settle on the far side of the sea,
> even there your hand will guide me,
>   your right hand will hold me fast.

If I say, 'Surely the darkness will hide me
  and the light become night around me,'
even the darkness will not be dark to you;
  the night will shine like the day,
  for darkness is as light to you. (vv.7–12)

There is nowhere we can go where God cannot see us. He tracks us all the time. He knows where we are because He is where we are. Theologians call this ability of the Almighty to be everywhere, omnipresence. Everywhere present.

I have always loved the story (which is supposed to be true) of an atheist who wrote on the steamed-up windows of a railway carriage the words 'God is nowhere'. As he sat back and looked at the words however he realised that he had put more of a gap than he had intended between two of the letters in the word 'nowhere' and it read, 'God is now here'. Such was the impact of this upon him that it led eventually to his conversion.

David also tells us that God knew us in our mother's womb.

For you created my inmost being;
  you knit me together in my mother's womb.
I praise you because I am fearfully and wonderfully made;
  your works are wonderful,
  I know that full well.
My frame was not hidden from you
  when I was made in the secret place.
When I was woven together in the depths of the earth,
  your eyes saw my unformed body.
All the days ordained for me

were written in your book
before one of them came to be. (vv.13–16)

We have been beginning to realise over the last few decades something of what goes on in the womb when a child is being formed. It's there that our characteristics and our talents are developed in such a unique way and where our individuality is shaped. I have always thought that if there were a flap in a woman's abdomen that she could lift and see how her unborn child were doing there would be far fewer abortions.

Permit this personal story. Two incidents took place close to each other when I was a young boy in school that left a deep impression on me; I was about 12 years of age at the time. The first was when the headmaster of my school, Danny Jones, came into the class and began handing out marked essays. He stopped at my desk and said to the whole class, 'Hughes has written one of the best essays I have ever read.' Later he took me into his private room and said, 'You know I think that one day you will become a writer.'

A few weeks later the games teacher for the school, Emrys Jones, said to me after I had been involved in a rugby match, 'Hughes, I think you might make a good rugby player one day.' Those two complimentary statements made within a few weeks of each other had different effects on me. The one about becoming a writer had a profound effect upon me; the one about becoming a good rugby player just a moderate effect. Why did the former have a deeper effect than the latter?

I think it was because I had heard something like that before. Where, you might ask? Will you think me somewhat whacky if I were to tell you it was in the womb? I believe with all my heart that while I was in the womb God was laying down in my personality the gifts and abilities that He knew I could best use for Him. And during the nine months I was there the Spirit was at work preparing me for the work He wanted me to do for Him during my time on earth.

The Spirit was saying something like this, 'You would make a terrible accountant and a very ineffective businessman but here's what I want you to do, I want you to write and speak for Me, and I am going to see to it that every incident, every failure, every setback, no matter what happens, they will not destroy what I desire for you. Even the worst stuff that happens to you is going to be redeemable and I am going to glorify My name in you.'

So when the headmaster said, 'I think you will make a writer', it was a word that reverberated within me for I had heard it before, not with my physical ears of course, but with the inner ears of my soul.

Consider this truth as it relates to your own life. I would be surprised if when you ponder it, your heart will not leap up in adoration and praise. When leading a seminar in Birmingham many years ago I made the point I am making here that God knew all about us when we were in our mother's womb. A woman came up to me in the interval and said somewhat excitedly, 'While you were talking about God knowing us in our mother's womb something was released in me that I just don't know how to describe. All my life I have focused on knowing God but the thought hit me like a thunderbolt as you were speaking – He knew me before I knew Him. It is on the basis of His knowledge of me that I can come to know Him.'

I had not quite seen the truth she was making in that light before and that evening on the drive back from Birmingham to my home in Surrey I let my mind engage with that truth: if God did not know me then I would never have been able to know Him. Mark Twain, the writer, said that he could live for a whole month on a single compliment. I lived for a whole month meditating on the truth that what matters supremely is not just that I know God (wonderful though that is) but the larger fact that He knows me. All my knowledge of Him depends on His sustained initiative in knowing me.

David continues:

> How precious to me are your thoughts, O God!
>   How vast is the sum of them!
> Were I to count them,
>   they would outnumber the grains of sand. (vv.17–18)

Of course the psalmist here is talking about God's thoughts as expressed through the works of His hands in creation. But I think we can deduce from this that His thoughts are towards us also. Beings made in the image of God are worth more to the Creator than a thousand galaxies. This might be difficult for some to understand but God's thoughts towards us are not occasional or infrequent, sporadic or intermittent. He thinks about us continuously. His thoughts towards His creation, says the psalmist, are more in number than the grains of sand – can we imagine how many are on the sea shores of the world? It is impossible to compute.

I remember years ago leading one of the CWR Holy Land tours and on the drive from Jerusalem to Galilee, a journey of several hours, I sat next to a girl who talked to me all the way about her fiancé who wasn't with her on the tour. As we talked, she kept looking at her watch. 'Excuse me,' she said, 'my boyfriend and I have a pact that on the hour and half hour whenever we are awake we think about each other for a minute.' The same thing happened half an hour later and so on until we arrived at our destination.

Well, be assured of this, the Almighty does not think of you only on the hour or the half hour; you are always on His mind. One would think that God has other things to ponder but the mind of the Eternal focuses on us more than anything else, I believe, because we human beings are the only ones in the whole of creation made in the divine image.

'When I awake I am still with you,' says David. The thought here is that the sleep of exhaustion overcomes every attempt to count God's thoughts, and waking only floods our soul once more with the sense of His presence and power and love for us.

Over the years, in talking with Christians about matters of the soul, I have listened to them say that though they know and understand intellectually that God loves them they somehow do not feel it in their emotions. This it seems is a problem for more believers than we might think. But how can it be overcome?

One of the ways which some have dealt with this problem is by locking into a law of the personality that works in this way: what we think about affects the way we feel and how we feel affects the way we act. In other words our emotions follow our thoughts like little ducks follow their mother on a pond. The more we think about something the more effect it will have on our feelings

Dr Martyn Lloyd-Jones in his book, The Sermon on the Mount, claims that often we have the wrong idea about faith. 'What do you think faith is?' he asks. Well, think about it for a moment. What is faith? Of course a dozen different definitions might spring into your mind, but listen to how Martyn Lloyd-Jones put it. 'Primarily faith,' he says, 'is thinking' (emphasis mine).

I must confess that the first time I read those words of Martyn Lloyd-Jones I sat up and took notice. I had never before considered faith to be thinking. But follow his reasoning and I think you will be convinced that the point he makes is indeed a valid one.

In chapter 6 of Matthew's Gospel Jesus tells His followers to

'Look at the birds of the air; they do not sow or reap or store away in barns, and yet your heavenly Father feeds them ... See how the lilies of the field grow. They do not labour or spin. Yet I tell you that not even Solomon in all his splendour was dressed like one of these. If that is how God clothes the grass of the field, which is here today and tomorrow is thrown into the fire, will he not much more clothe you, O you of little faith?' (vv.26–30)

Martyn Lloyd-Jones commenting on these words of Jesus says that what our Lord is doing here is telling His listeners that the reason they have little faith is because they do not think. He says: 'Look at the birds, our Lord is saying, think about them – and draw your deductions. Look at the lilies of the field how they grow, think about them – and draw your deductions. Look at the grass in the fields, think about it – and draw your deductions.' The more we ponder the goodness of God and His ability to take care of His creation, the more we think about that, the more our faith will flourish.

It is the same in relation to this matter of feeling God's love streaming into our emotions. The more we think of how God thinks of us the more our feelings will get the message. And how does the Almighty think of us? With love and affection. Search out the many scriptures where God spells out His love for His children. Ponder them, meditate on them, think on them and you will discover as thousands have before you that the more you think about how God thinks about you the more your feelings will be affected.

Not so long ago when I was feeling that God seemed far away I reflected on the scripture: 'Can a mother forget the baby at her breast and have no compassion on the child she has borne? Though she may forget, I will not forget you!' (Isa. 49:15). As I thought about the fact that God cannot forget me it was not long before tears began to fill my eyes.

There was a story in the papers the other day of a footballer who over a year ago went to visit a dying child who doted on him. He took a football with his signature on it and gave it to the child. The press were there and he had his photograph taken with the child and articles appeared the next day in the newspapers applauding him for his concern. Months later when being interviewed by the press over another matter someone said, 'How is the little boy you visited who was dying?' The footballer confessed that he had forgotten all about the visit, but to his credit appeared suitably sad about his forgetfulness.

As a child of God be assured that God will never forget you. Others may forget you, forget your birthday, forget something you did, forget your name even. But God never forgets and, what is more, thinks about you continually.

There is not a moment when His eye is off me or His attention distracted from me. I am never out of His mind. Blessed be His holy name!

You might have noticed that the psalmist began his psalm by acknowledging that God knew everything about Him, but now he ends it by asking that God would help him know himself. David is opening himself up to God and asking that the Almighty would put His spotlight on anything in his heart that might be offensive or hinder his communication with the Eternal. He longs that if there is any hindrance in him it might be revealed and put away.

A more modern day writer put that same thought in these words:

Jesus the hindrance show,
Which I have feared to see
Yet let me now consent to know
What keeps me out of Thee.

God never rejects this kind of plea.

Would you be surprised when I tell you that Psalm 139 is my most favourite of all the psalms? I revel in the thought that God knows me so intimately that He can take care of me perfectly. The fact that I am always on His mind is one of the great driving forces of my life.

A God like this can have my heart any time.

~10~

OUR TRUE COUNTRY

REVELATION 21 & 22

Then I saw a new heaven and a new earth, for the first heaven and the first earth had passed away, and there was no longer any sea. I saw the Holy City, the new Jerusalem, coming down out of heaven from God, prepared as a bride beautifully dressed for her husband. (21:1–2)

Ever since I began to travel to different parts of the world in the service of Jesus Christ, I have always tried to learn as much as I can about the country I plan to visit before the journey actually begins. That is why I have a section of my library given over entirely to guide books to various countries and they have all received preliminary study before I have set foot in any of the distant lands.

Some day in the not too distant future God will give me leave to depart this world and in the knowledge of that, I have spent a good deal of my time in recent years focusing on just what awaits me on the other side.

And more than any other book of the Bible the book of Revelation has helped me in this regard. Nowhere do we read anything more beautiful about what lies on the other side than John's description of it in the last two chapters of Revelation.

Trying to depict the glories of heaven is like attempting to describe to unborn children some of the sights and sounds they will encounter when they leave the womb and enter the big wide world. I get the feeling as I read these two final chapters of Revelation that he is struggling to tell the untellable and he has to ransack his vocabulary to paint a verbal picture for us of the glories of another world.

I remember reading many years ago of about a ten-year-old girl who was born blind, but through a radical and new operation was able to see. As the bandages were taken off her eyes she looked out into the hospital garden, saw the green fields, the lake, the flowers and the trees and she clapped her hands in glee and said, 'O Mother, why didn't you tell me it was so beautiful?' 'My darling,' said her mother, 'I tried ... oh how I tried ... but I just didn't have the words.'

This I feel is John's predicament as he writes in these closing chapters concerning the joys and delights of heaven. He just doesn't have the words. He pushes language to its utmost limit as he focuses on trying to explain what heaven is like. Of course Christians have differing views concerning John's description of heaven in Revelation as to whether it is metaphorical or literal. All through my Christian life I have vacillated on this issue but there is one thing I am certain about and it is this – however we view it, heaven is grander and greater and more glorious than any human words or descriptions can convey.

John begins by telling us: 'I saw the Holy City, the New Jerusalem, coming down out of heaven from God like a bride beautifully dressed for her husband' (v.2). And when it comes to describing the details of the New Jerusalem it seems as if his pen is ablaze. The verses from chapter 21 and part of chapter 22 are breathtaking in their beauty, and cascade in a way that fires the imagination. It certainly fires mine. What I would like to do now is to share with you the five most exciting things that thrill me with the prospect of going to heaven.

Most people I find want to go to heaven but not just yet. A Christian getting on in age described it in this way: 'I am sitting in the departure lounge of life hoping that the plane will be very much delayed.' I have always loved the story of the pastor who when asked to speak to the children before they left the service for their Sunday School classes began by saying, 'How many of you would like to go to heaven?' Everyone put up their hands except one little boy on the front row and when the pastor said, 'What! You don't want to go to heaven when you die?' the little boy replied, 'Oh, when I die. I thought you meant right now!'

There are of course much more than five things that can be drawn from these chapters but let me select what to me are the five most significant.

The first thing that strikes me about John's description of heaven is the absence of the things that have been so hurtful and upsetting on earth. He identifies four things that will not be there: there will be no more death, no more mourning, no more crying and no more pain. These four things sum up most of the trials and difficulties we face on this earth. Many at some time or another have had to face the death of a loved one and mourn their passing. And only those who have passed through that trial know how devastating it can be. Well, be assured of this, says John, there will be no death in heaven. No funeral train ever snakes along those winding hills.

There will be no crying there either. No shedding of tears. I wonder how many tears you have shed in your life? How many of you have cried yourself to sleep at night because of some bitter disappointment, betrayal, hurt, the unfaithfulness of a spouse, rejection or just perhaps because you felt worthless alongside others who seem to have more gifts and talents than you? Well, know this, in heaven the great handkerchief of love will be taken out and every tear will be wiped away. There will be no need for tears because the cause of tears will have been forever removed.

And what about pain? Having endured a great deal of pain in the last few years because of my prostate cancer the idea of a painless world greatly appeals to me I can tell you. Whatever pains you have carried in your life, whether they be emotional or physical remember this – you will never feel pain in heaven.

But there will be something else missing also in heaven. There will be no sin. John tells us: '... the cowardly, the unbelieving, the vile, the murderers, the sexually immoral, those who practise magic arts, the idolaters and all liars – their place will be in the fiery lake of burning sulphur' (v.8).

Aren't you sickened by the sleaze and filth that faces us every day in this world? Sometimes as I open my newspaper or watch reports on television or hear of the most blatant sins and iniquities practised by some in today's society I find myself feeling physically sick.

The second thing that intrigues me as I read John's description of heaven is the fact that the New Jerusalem has twelve gates.
Three gates to the East, three gates to the North, three gates to the South and three gates to the West. Twelve gates to glory. Do you know what this suggests to me? The catholicity of the Christian faith; the embracing of the whole body of Christians, irrespective of denomination or theological persuasion. The gates point in all directions: East, North, West and South. Gates! Gates! Gates! Everywhere gates. It reminds me of that great hymn:

> In Christ there is no East or West,
> In Him no North or South
> But one great fellowship of love,
> Throughout the whole wide earth.

The clear meaning of the text is that the gates of heaven are open to men and women from all parts of the earth. All may come. 'Red and yellow, and black and white, says an old children's chorus, 'all are precious in His sight'. They truly are.

Look with me for a moment at the fact *there are three gates to the East*. The East speaks of a new day. Sunrise! This takes my mind to those who are on the first steps and stages of life – the young. Youth is the time when people seek to find meaning and purpose for their lives. If there is one thing for which I am thankful above all others in my life it is that I came to Christ when I was young. The greatest night of my life is when I walked down the aisle of a little Mission Hall in Wales, knelt at the front, surrendered my life to the Saviour and, to my astonishment, He forgave me all my sin and has sent my happy soul singing down the years.

There are three gates also to the North. What comes to mind when you think of the North? It is out of the North that the biting and bitter winds come. It is the place of harsh cold unrelenting gales. There are many people in the world who go through life having to handle more than their share of the cold winds of life. I have met many of them in my time. How wonderful it is to point them to the fact that Christ is a shelter from the fierce storms of life and enables us to deal with every wind of difficulty that comes?

Then again there are three gates to the South. The picture that comes to mind when we mention the word South is of balmy breezes, calm seas, blue skies, where the barometer always points to 'fair'. There are men and women in this world whose lives have been set amongst comfort, even luxury, and seem to have no need for anything. These are the people who concern me the most. They are the self-sufficient, the smug, the self-satisfied. The young cry out for meaning, the suffering cry out for relief but these people cry out for nothing. Yet there is a place even for them if they will yield themselves to the Saviour. His arms are open wide even to these.

Then finally there are three gates to the West. The West is where the sun sets. It pictures the dying of the day. I am thinking now of those in their sunset years who wonder what lies beyond the sunset. Thank God, the gates of glory are open to them too. Even though people spurn the offer of Christ in their youth or middle years His grace is sufficient to accept them even when they turn to Him when there are few years on earth still left.

So there it is – all may come. The Gates of Glory are open to everyone and there is no one on any part of Planet Earth who will be refused admission to heaven, providing they don't try to get in some other way, but enter in by the Gate.

The third thing that intrigues me about John's description of heaven is that he tells us the gates of the city are made of pearls.

Now a pearl is a wonderful thing. Scientists tell us that a pearl is a product of pain. Sometimes the pain is caused by the entry of a microscopic worm or a grain of sand that gets washed into the heart of an oyster. Immediately all the resources of the tiny organism rush to the spot where the breach has been made. The oyster exudes a precious secretion in order to close the breach and save its life. The foreign irritant is covered over and the wound is healed – by a pearl. It is true to say that where there is no pain there is no pearl.

Can you see the beautiful symbolism of all this? We enter into the New Jerusalem through the pains of the Saviour. There are many people today in our churches who argue that the death of our Lord Jesus Christ was unnecessary and they preach that God can forgive without the cross. They do not pause to explain why Christ should endure, as God, something which was quite unnecessary. They support their view by quoting the story of the parable of the Prodigal Son and they point out that when the prodigal was penitent and came home his father ran to meet him and forgive him.

There was no talk of atonement in the story, they say. The elder brother did not have to bear some punishment before the prodigal could be forgiven. The Father met penitence with pardon and that is the picture of God's dealings with sinners. All we have to do is say sorry and it is all forgiven.

But the parable of the Prodigal Son is not a complete picture of God's relationship with His wayward children. It was not meant to be. The story is meant to convey the eagerness of God to save and His readiness to reconcile. We have to lay that story against other parts of Scripture and consider texts such as this: '... without the shedding of blood there is no forgiveness' (Heb. 9:22).

I often wonder if those in our churches who deny Christ's atonement are motivated by the fact that they do not like to think that the price of their salvation has already been paid. As John Stott puts it: 'Proud human beings would give anything to earn their own salvation or if they cannot earn it at least contribute to it and when they are told it is a non contributory gift of God, absolutely free and utterly undeserved, it is extremely humiliating to people's arrogant self-confidence.'

When Jesus went to the cross He was saying in effect: 'I am here because of you. You could not pay the price of redemption but I will pay it for you.' The cross humbles us and shows us that God in Christ did for us what we could not do for ourselves. If we do not receive salvation as a free gift then we do not receive it all!

So the message of those gates of pearl is this – we cannot scale those jasper walls; we have to go in through the gates made of pearl. The entrance to the New Jerusalem is through the hurts and wounds of our Saviour, the Lord Jesus Christ.

The fourth thing I find intriguing about heaven is the fact that the city is awash with light.

It does not need the sun or the moon to shine on it, we are told, for 'the glory of God gives it light and the Lamb is its lamp' (v.23). Light is our fundamental visual experience; without light we could see nothing at all. The first work of creation, you remember, was the making of light.

Heaven is awash with brightness. As one preacher puts it: 'the light of heaven is not produced by 40-watt bulbs or even 100-watt bulbs hanging naked throughout the city; it is ablaze with the light that comes from God Himself'.

There is a connection I believe between the fact that heaven is awash with light and the foundation of 12 precious stones, which John mentioned earlier (21:19). Light, we are told by our scientists, is a gathering of colours, the stones separate the colours and hold them up, one by one, for emphasis and praise. I am indebted to Eugene Peterson here for the thought that precious stones go beyond affirming the light; they show its plenitude also.

'Precious stones', says Peterson 'are precious not because of their cost but because of their capacity to show off colour'. 'Light', he says,

comes to us in a fusion of colours. As it strikes objects some of the colours are absorbed and others reflected back to us. By the time the light gets to our retinas, bounced off skin or bark or flower, the edge has been taken off the original brightness. But certain stones do the opposite, they select particular colours out of the general light and present them to our eyes with an intense and burning purity.

Peterson points out also that some artists do something similar with their paints. Van Gogh, for example, makes us aware of yellow as we have never seen it before. The 12 stones which are the foundation of the New Jerusalem do this, they separate the colours of light and show them more purely.

I don't know if I am talking to someone now who because of the troubles and trials you have gone through, you feel that life here on this earth is a very monochrome existence. If so then take heart – in heaven it will all be different. If I might quote Peterson again: 'In heaven's light,' he says, 'we shall not only see objects but see also their dazzling light-charged beauty.' The place God has reserved for His blood-washed people is awash with an exuberant Niagara of colour. Never again will we have to put up with a monochrome existence. We are headed for a city of endless joys and delights, not the least being the enjoyment of colours such as we have never known here on earth.

The fifth and final thing – and perhaps the most exciting of all that I find intriguing about heaven is that Jesus is there.

I like what John says in 22:4 where he says simply but powerfully: 'they *will see his face.*' I have often wondered what the face of Jesus looks like. I have never been impressed with the faces of Jesus painted by artists throughout the centuries. All of them to my mind have something missing. That includes the many films that have been made about Jesus with modern-day actors.

I think the nearest I have ever come to what I expect the face of Jesus to look like is the Visual Bible presentation of the Gospel of Matthew. The actor's name is Bruce Marciano. There is something about his face; I think it is the joy on his countenance, that for me at least, gets closest to how I imagine our Lord must have appeared.

Many have suggested that our Lord's face would have been serious, basing it on the text: 'He was a man of sorrows and acquainted with grief.' But I think we need to set against that fact the truth also that the fruit of the Spirit is joy and, believing as I do that Jesus exemplified all the fruit of the Spirit, surely joy must have emanated from Him also.

There are two things about Jesus that I long to experience: to hear His voice and to see His face. A song we used to sing in my home church when I was a boy was this:

> The Bride eyes not her garment
> But her dear Bridegroom's face
> I will not gaze at glory but on my King of Grace
> Not at the gifts He giveth
> But at His nailed pierced hands
> The Lamb is all the glory in Immanuel's land.

C.S. Lewis in his book *Till We Have Faces* tells the story of a queen called Orual who felt she was so ugly that she wore a veil and when she hid behind that veil she didn't know who she was. It was only when she took the veil off that she became a real person.

In a sense, all of us here on earth have a veil over our faces and we will never fully become the person God meant us to be or fully know ourselves until we look upon His face. I shall never forget when just after the Second World War, King George came on a tour through the valleys of Wales and drove at one point through the little village where I lived. Everyone in the village lined the roads to watch the king pass slowly and wave to us from his open-topped car.

The following Sunday our pastor David Thomas asked the congregation: 'How many of you saw the king the other day?' Everyone raised their hands. 'And were you changed by the sight?' he asked. 'No,' we all responded. He said, 'But when you see Jesus you will be changed,' and quoting the text 1 Corinthians 13:12, said, 'Now we see but a poor reflection as in a mirror; then we shall see face to face. Now I know in part; then I shall know fully, even as I am fully known.'

I can promise you this, every one of us when we get to heaven is going to have a face lift! We don't really have faces now. What we have is the potential for a face which will be completed and realised only when we gaze upon His face.

A few years ago I visited a man who was dying and as we talked about heaven he confessed to me that he was feeling somewhat scared about dying. 'Tell me, what are you scared about?' I asked. 'I suppose it is that I don't know much about what lies beyond the grave,' he replied. 'I have never really given much thought to the content of heaven ... can you tell me what you know about that?'

I said I did not know much about the content of heaven – what was there, but I did know who was there. And as we talked about the fact that Jesus was there, the Saviour whom he had trusted, his voice took on a new note and a look of reassurance grew on his countenance. Before I left we sang together the words of an old hymn:

My knowledge of that life is small
  The eye of faith is dim
But 'tis enough that Christ knows all
  And I shall be with Him.

People often talk about heaven in terms of meeting up with loved ones who have gone on before, and wonderful though that will be, surely the greatest delight and attraction of heaven is meeting face to face with Jesus.

I have always loved C.S. Lewis's term for heaven. He calls it our 'our true country'– the title I have chosen for this message. 'Heaven is the place we were really made for,' says Lewis. 'Heaven was not made for us, we are made for heaven.'

Let me end with this story. One of our great Welsh preachers was preaching one day on the subject of heaven. His eloquence and passion was so stirring that a man sitting on the back row moved forward to the next seat. As the preacher continued with his stirring eloquence and descriptions of heaven, the man moved forward seat by seat, albeit unconsciously, until he was soon sitting on the front row. Coming to the end of his sermon, the preacher closed his eyes and said, 'Friends, I feel that heaven is so close to us tonight that there is no more than the thickness of a pane of glass between us.' At this point the man sitting on the front row stood up and shouted, 'Well put your fist through it man!'

I think that sums up my thoughts on the subject also.

Roll on eternity when, above all things, we shall see our Saviour's face. And where every chapter will be better than the one before.

What a day that will be. More and more I find myself praying along these lines: O Day of rest and gladness delay not thy dawning. Let the angels be sent forth to gather the elect. Let the promises be proclaimed that bear in their train these matchless glories.

Even so, come Lord Jesus!

~ 11 ~

BREAD ENOUGH
AND TO SPARE

LUKE 15:17

'How many of my father's hired servants have bread enough and to spare ...' (NKJV)

The parables of Jesus are like diamonds; there are so many fascinating sides to them. Many years ago there used to be a shop in Regent Street, London, where at various appointed times you could watch a diamond being cut. After attending one of these cutting sessions I came away feeling it had been one of the most fascinating few hours of my life.

A man who cuts diamonds is called a lapidary and as the one I watched worked on the diamond, he kept up a constant commentary on what he was doing. 'A diamond,' he said, 'is a crystal, a prism that reflects light and disperses it. In this particular diamond I am aiming to cut many facets but one central face so that the light falls from the facets on to the central face and hence out on to people's appreciative gaze.'

Jesus cut His parables like that. There are many facets to them but just one central face. How many times have you heard a sermon on the Prodigal Son which has dealt with some facet of the parable, such as his foolishness in spending everything he had in riotous living, or the pettiness of the older brother? But those things are not where the heart of the story lies. The central face of the parable is to be found in these words:

But while he was still a long way off, his father saw him and was filled with compassion for him; he ran to his son, threw his arms around him and kissed him.

The father ... ran.

That is the main message Jesus is trying to convey in this parable. Consider the context with me for a moment. The chapter begins with the Pharisees accusing Jesus of receiving sinners and eating with them. It was this statement that led to Jesus telling three stories, one about a lost coin, another about a lost sheep and the third about a lost son.

Underlying all these stories is the compelling truth that God takes the initiative in redemption. The Pharisees would be willing to accept someone who had taken himself in hand and sought to amend his life, but the glory of Christ's gospel is that it has a welcome for the deepest-dyed sinners and undertakes to do for them what they cannot do for themselves. That is what makes the gospel different from every other religion.

It was said by Aristotle, the ancient Greek philosopher, that it was the mark of a great man that he did not run. Such haste was considered unseemly in anyone who had some standing in society. Yet here in the parable of the Prodigal Son, Jesus is calmly telling us that no sooner does a prodigal put his feet on the road towards home than God Himself does not consider it beneath His dignity to run to meet him!

The central face of the parable then is this: God is ready to reconcile and eager to save. The Almighty hastens to greet us in our guilt and shame. Now having made clear the central face of the parable I want, if I may, to focus on one of its facets. It is the one found in the words of my text:

There is bread enough and to spare in my Father's house ...

When we focus on the question: what really brought the prodigal home, surely there is only one answer. He was *hungry*. And he knew a place where there was an abundance of bread.

That was the one thing above all others that acted like a magnet to his soul. He could not be sure of his father's forgiveness or that he would be restored to his former position but there was one thing he was sure of – there was bread in his father's house *and to spare*.

Now let me lift this thought to what might be considered a daring level. Bread is used in the Bible as a type of several things. Our Lord once declared, 'I am the bread of life' (John 6:35). It is also a type of the Christian Church. The apostle Paul, when addressing the Corinthians converts, said, 'For we, being many, are one bread ...' (1 Cor. 10:17, NKJV).

I do not think I am being too fanciful when I extend the apostle's thought of the Church being 'one bread' to suggest that part of the Church's purpose here on earth is not simply to enjoy and celebrate the togetherness that comes from being in Christ, but to share that joy with others. To put it another way: It is not enough to have bread for ourselves. The vital question is: Do we have enough to spare?

Permit me to dwell on that question for a little while.

IF WE FOLLOW THE NEW TESTAMENT PATTERN WE *SHOULD* HAVE ENOUGH TO SPARE

Whenever I turn over the pages of the Gospels and the epistles it becomes blazingly clear that the message of evangelism throbs on every page. My old pastor (the man who led me to Christ and mentored me in the days following my conversion) used to say, 'You have been saved to serve. Seek now to win someone else to Christ.'

The New Testament fairly bulges with accounts of people who, having been introduced to Jesus, race to tell others about Him. Take Andrew, for example, one of Jesus' first disciples. No sooner did he find Christ than he hastened to tell his brother Peter about Him which resulted in Simon Peter becoming one of the most prominent and productive of the 12 disciples.

Think, too, of the woman at the well who ran fleet-footed to tell others of the Saviour. And of the many other personalities in the Gospels as well as the rest of the New Testament who, having met the Saviour, were gripped with a desire to tell others about Him. The instinct of every newborn soul is to share what they have received with others. It's a tragedy that so many suppress that instinct and remain like the artic rivers – frozen at the mouth.

Evangelism has been described as 'one beggar telling another where to find bread'. Not to tell a hungry and starving world where they can find bread to satisfy their souls is criminal.

Soul winning is a biblical imperative.

One of the problems of today's Church (generally speaking) is the fact that, albeit unnoticed, evangelism is receiving less and less emphasis and is falling out of favour. The urgency of soul winning taught so clearly in the New Testament is no longer being emphasised in the way it once was.

As a firsthand observer of the Christian Church for over 60 years I fear something rather strange and sinister is happening in our midst. There are exceptions to what I am saying of course but it seems that attempts to convert other people are being seen by many of today's Christians as a gross infringement of people's individual liberties and a most distasteful form of arrogance.

In many churches some of their members are completely indifferent to the need for evangelism while others are actively resistant to it. How can one faith religion claim a monopoly on truth? some ask. Are there not different ways to God? What right have we to interfere in other people's privacy or attempt to impose our views on them? Let's rather mind our own business and devoutly hope that other people will mind theirs.

A research conducted amongst several thousand evangelical young people in the USA asked this one question: 'What do you regard as the central text of Scripture?' If that question had been asked of young people in my day the answer would have been John 3:16. Ninety-five per cent, however, answered, 'Judge not that you be not judged'.

What accounts for this change amongst the youth of our day? I believe it is because a concept has swept the world that presents one of the greatest threats and challenges to the cause of Christ in any part of history. That concept is – *tolerance*. It's part of this postmodern age to be tolerant of other people's religion and not to say that Christianity is better than any other faith.

But Christianity, as the late Archbishop William Temple said, 'is a profoundly intolerant religion'. There are not many ways to heaven; there is just one. There can be no tolerance in mathematics, no tolerance in physics, no tolerance in charting a path to the moon, and no tolerance when it comes to the way of salvation: '... for there is no other name under heaven given to men by which we must be saved' (Acts 4:12).

In the face of that text, believing that there is more than one way to heaven is as foolish as thinking that by taking your mobile phone and dialling any number will connect you to your home.

Let us never forget that the two main illustrations of soul winning in the New Testament are that of a fisherman and a shepherd; so you see, souls must be saved by hook or by crook! And let us never forget also that the very first two letters of the gospel being GO, means that there is always a GO in the gospel.

IF THE WORLD IS TO BE WON TO GOD THEN WE *MUST* HAVE ENOUGH TO SPARE

Some years ago, during the late twentieth century, a Christian magazine researched what was the favourite illustration of preachers. As you can imagine there were thousands of submissions but one kept coming up time and time again which eventually won first place in the list.

This is that story.

After our Lord returned to heaven, following His death and resurrection, He was asked by the angels what arrangements He had made for the propagation of the gospel on earth. The Lord replied that he had commissioned His disciples to carry the gospel to the ends of the earth by word of mouth, at the same time being examples of the truth they presented.

One of the angels said, 'But Lord, these men and women are fallible and prone to weaknesses ... what if for some reason they fail to follow your plan? Surely You have some alternative arrangements for the propagation of the gospel should these men and women not be up to the task?'

The Lord looked at the angels and said solemnly, 'If they do not fulfil the task I have given them then the work will simply not get done. *I have no other plan.'*

It has been said that there are just three ways by which the gospel can be presented to the world. Firstly, through personal evangelism, one person telling another. Secondly, through mass evangelism – an evangelist (such as Billy Graham) preaching to large crowds. Thirdly, evangelism through the local church.

John Stott says that local church evangelism 'is the most normal natural and productive method of spreading the gospel today'. The church at Thessalonica is a great example of this. Paul tells them in 1 Thessalonians 1:5–8 that the gospel came to them with power and they became a model to all the believers in Macedonia and Achaia because, as he put it: 'The Lord's message rang out from you not only in Macedonia and Achaia – your faith in God has become known everywhere.'

Listen again to the phrase: *'The Lord's message rang out from you ...'* It conjures up a picture of believers sounding out the gospel with energy, fervour and great enthusiasm. The church in Thessalonica not only heard the gospel but passed it on. And that is the duty of every local church. *This is God's principal form of evangelism and if that had been done in the way it should be done then Britain would have long ago been evangelised.* And what is true of Britain is also true of many other parts of the world.

I remember around the late 1980s preaching one Sunday in a church on the South coast of England and after coming away saying to myself, 'That is the deadest and coldest church I think I have ever preached in in my life'. Years later I was invited back to that church, to find that it had been transformed.

The service throbbed with life, the congregation were radiant with happiness, the place was crowded with young people, the music was wonderful and the presence of God most powerful. During lunch with the pastor I tentatively raised the issue of what was the explanation for the different atmosphere in the church compared to my last visit. 'What accounts for this?' I asked. The pastor then told me this story.

'Not long after your last visit,' he said, 'a tragic thing happened in our church that brought us to our knees in repentance. A young girl, heaving pregnant and without a wedding ring on her finger, came to our Sunday night services for a couple of weeks, but no one spoke to her or tried to befriend her. We didn't see her any more for a while and then one night she threw herself off a cliff overlooking the sea, and in the morning someone found her body spiked on a jagged rock. When a photograph of her appeared in the local paper we remembered that she had visited our church for a couple of Sundays but what sent us to our knees in deep repentance was the fact the newspaper reported that in her hand was a crumpled-up note on which were the words "*nobody cared*".

'The whole church realised we had failed this girl by not being alert to the needs of newcomers to our church and the knowledge of our failure led us first to ask God's forgiveness and then change our ways. We spent weeks in prayer and repentance and vowed we would never let that happen again. From that day to this we have not only welcomed newcomers to our church but we go out to seek them and bring them in. It is sad that this had to happen to make us aware of our inwardness and our uncaring attitudes but, to answer your question, this is the explanation for the great change you notice in our midst.'

Then, having heard me once preach on the theme I am focusing on now, he said somewhat wistfully, 'We were a church then who had bread but not enough to spare.'

I have to admit that I wasn't very interested in finishing my lunch after listening to that moving story. We ended up, the pastor and myself, on our knees before God asking Him to give us an even greater passion for souls and a deeper longing to bring others to the Saviour.

Many churches today (thankfully not all) resemble the local golf club. Their common interest of course happens to be God rather than golf, but they see themselves as religious people doing religious things together. They concentrate on the benefits of membership and have never understood, as Archbishop William Temple said, that 'the Church is the only co-operative society in the world which exists for the benefit of its non-members'. Temple was using a hyperbole of course as he would be the first to agree that Christians do have a responsibility to each other to love one another and encourage one another. But, that said, far too many churches are totally introverted like an ingrown toenail.

One writer I came across who has his finger on the pulse of twenty-first-century charismatic Christianity said, 'For many people today church is about (1) obtaining financial prosperity, (2) securing a personal "breakthrough" and (3) finding the key to getting your prayers answered.' He added, 'I'm amazed we don't end up every service by singing four verses of "It's all about me, Lord, it's all about me".'

I said a moment ago that if the local church had done its job in the way it should be done then large areas of the world would be evangelised by now. What an indictment that is against us and how it ought to send us to our knees in fervent believing prayer for God to deepen our passion for souls and give the world the impression that in the Father's house there is not just bread but enough to spare.

IF WE PLACE OURSELVES AFRESH IN GOD'S HANDS THEN WE *WILL* HAVE ENOUGH TO SPARE

There are some things in life which when broken bring great sadness and sorrow. Break a beautiful vase and the damage is irreparable. Break a deep friendship and the relationship may never again be restored. But there are things in life too that are made to be broken. Take, for example, a lark's egg. How lovely it looks. How exquisite in shape and shade! You hold the tiny fragile thing in your hand and you think to yourself what a shame it is that it has to be broken. Yet you know that if the shell is not broken the lark will never sing at the door of heaven; the imprisoned music will remain forever mute!

Bread is one of the things that's made to be broken also. Left to itself it grows a green beard and goes bad. Then it has to be thrown out – uneaten. Christians both individually and corporately are made to be broken too. Not by factions and schisms and secessions – but broken in spirit and contrite in heart before God.

How willing are we to put ourselves in the hands of the Master and allow Him to break us – break us of our pride, our self-centredness, our stubborn commitment to independence and our desire to take our own way in preference to His? The psalmist in Psalm 51 cried, 'The sacrifices of God are a broken spirit; a broken and contrite heart, O God, you will not despise' (v.17). That must be our prayer too if we are to be used by the Lord.

It's an interesting thing that whenever we see Jesus taking bread in His hands in the Gospels He always broke it. He did so at the miracle of the feeding of the 5,000. The second time He took bread in His hands and broke it was at the Last Supper. And the third time was when He broke bread with the two disconsolate disciples on the road to Emmaus, recorded for us in Luke 24.

Have you heard the story of Ignatius, one of the Early Church Fathers, who was flung to a savage beast in an arena before the eyes of gaping thousands? The statement he made at that moment lives on: 'I am the grain of God,' he cried. 'I must be ground between the lion's teeth to make bread for His people.' It is unlikely that you or I will ever have to meet such a fate but brokenness in one degree or another is what we must experience if we are to be broken bread for the world. Paradoxically, it is only as we are broken that the world can be made whole.

If you will permit a personal testimony at this point, over the past couple of decades situations have happened in my life that have in turn transformed me. First my wife died with cancer. Three weeks later I lost my father to a massive heart attack. Some years later and within ten months of each other I lost my only two sons, David and John, one to a liver disease and the other to a heart attack. In between these difficult situations I was diagnosed with prostate cancer which has now spread to the bones in my right leg. This has meant endless visits to hospitals and great restrictions on my ministry.

At times it seemed as if huge pieces were being broken off me and I wondered what would come of it all. However, I have come to see that out of that brokenness has come a new note in my ministry that those who know me closely have commented on time and time again. There is a softness in me that wasn't quite there before, a new understanding of those who suffer, a new appreciation of God's wonderful grace and a deep desire to share with others the things that God has shared with me in the midst of my sufferings.

At the love feasts of the Early Church the following beautiful prayer incorporated in the *Didache* or *Teaching of the Twelve Apostles* was frequently offered:

> We thank Thee Father for this broken bread which was scattered upon the hills and being gathered together became one. So let Thy Church be gathered from the ends of the earth into Thy Kingdom.

Out of our Saviour's brokenness have come endless and eternal blessings. We must not shrink from the breaking process either. As one Christian poet put it:

It is the way the Master went
Should not the servant tread it still?

My dear friends in Jesus, let us not forget that outside in the world are poor famished prodigals who are hungry for the bread that comes down from heaven. Where can they find it?

Only in and through the Church.

But when they look towards the Church what do they see? A Church split by factions, insulated, isolated and inward-looking, more concerned about political structures than in reaching out to others.

Whatever things have been like in the Church over previous times, may God so touch our hearts that our concern for others will be greater than the concern we have for ourselves and that this attitude will come across to the world in all we say and do. Then maybe there will be those – multitudes of them perhaps – who, when realising their spiritual hunger, will look towards the Church and say: 'They seem to have the bread I am searching for in abundance. I'm heading for the Father's House.'

~12~

GOD'S RECIPE
FOR REVIVAL

2 CHRONICLES 7:14

'... if my people, who are called by my name, will humble themselves and pray and seek my face and turn from their wicked ways, then will I hear from heaven and will forgive their sin and will heal their land.'

There is, I believe, no more crucial issue facing the Church of Jesus Christ at this time in its history than the subject of Holy Spirit revival. And there is no greater passage in the whole of Scripture that shows the way to revival than this passage found in 2 Chronicles 7:14. Most Christians are familiar with it and can recite it word for word. It is God's final and finished formula on the subject; His recipe for a spiritual awakening.

But what really is revival? Revival is a very difficult word to define. Revival in a definition is like David in Saul's armour. It just doesn't fit. There is too much of God in it. There have been many definitions but when they are all finished it remains one of heaven's greatest mysteries. Out of the many attempted definitions I have come across, the ones I like best are these:

D.M. Panton says: 'Revival is the inrush of divine life into a body threatening to become a corpse.' Christmas Evans, one of our great Welsh preachers, said: 'Revival is God bending down to the dying embers of a fire just about to go out and breathing into it until it bursts again into flame.' My old pastor used to say 'Revival is waking up to the fact that you are asleep.' He used to say that many Christians are afflicted with a sleeping sickness and they don't know they are asleep until they wake up. Can it be that we can be afflicted with a sleeping sickness and even though we attend church, sing, raise our hands, we can be asleep to our real spiritual condition?

My favourite definition of revival is the simple but sublime statement of Dr Martyn Lloyd-Jones: 'Revival,' he said, 'is the Church returning to Pentecost.'

When Billy Graham conducted a tent crusade in Los Angeles in the late 1940s, as a young Youth For Christ evangelist, thousands of people came to Christ, many of them Hollywood film stars. The liberal churches (liberalism is the mindset that puts human thoughts above God's thoughts) said, 'Billy Graham has put the Church back 100 years.' When he heard that, Billy is said to have responded: 'Oh dear ... I was really trying to put it back 2,000 years.'

At Pentecost a powerful surge of spiritual energy and supernatural power flowed into the midst of those early disciples such as had never been known before. It was more than a trickle, more than a rivulet, more even than a river. It was a mighty Niagara of God's blessing that flooded the Early Church in such a way that its impact upon the world was quite staggering. A return to Pentecost is without doubt our greatest need.

Nowadays I am afraid we tend to call anything a revival. The word is used so loosely that it is in danger of losing its true meaning. A pastor said we had a revival in our church last Sunday – six people were converted. Now that is wonderful, but it is not revival. My concern is that if we use the word revival too loosely then it can mislead us into understanding what true revival is all about. We may easily settle for less than God wants to give us.

Many mistake a great evangelistic thrust for revival. For example, when Billy Graham came to Britain in the early 1950s, and thousands were converted, some of the Christian newspapers said, 'Revival is here.'

But it wasn't revival in the true sense of the word. It was God-blessed evangelism. Evangelism is the expression of the Church. Revival is an experience in the Church. In evangelism a preacher calls on people to be converted; in revival people cry out 'What must I do to be saved?' When people experience a series of exciting meetings that is dubbed revival. But again revival results in exciting meetings but exciting meetings are not in themselves revival.

So how do we move towards revival? That's where I must bring you face to face with my text. What I want to do with this text is to turn it phrase by phrase in the same way that a diamond cutter would do with a diamond so that the light shines from every facet of it. The text lies in Scripture like a diamond on a velvet couch and it never ceases to glisten and glitter as the light of the Holy Spirit falls upon it. My prayer is that this great text will do for you what it has done for me and set your heart on fire for revival. Now note how it begins – with the preposition 'if'.

'IF ...'

A preposition, it has been said, can alter a proposition. And nowhere is that more evident than in the opening word of this most marvellous text. Just as great doors swing open on small hinges, so this word unfolds for us the way to revival.

'If' is always a word of condition. Take this for example: 'If anyone is thirsty, let him come to me, and drink' (John 7:37). Or: 'If you do not forgive men their sins, your Father will not forgive your sins' (Matt. 6:15). The Bible fairly bulges with texts in which God implies that if we will do this He will do that. So clearly, right at the start, some responsibility is placed at our door. God will do His part if we are willing to do ours. So you see, a lot depends on that word if: it tells us that whatever part a sovereign God plays in a spiritual re-awakening, we have a part to play too.

But to whom is God speaking in this passage of Scripture?

'IF MY PEOPLE ...'

Revival begins then with the people of God. You can't apply the word 'revival' to non-Christians. Non-Christians don't need revival; they need a resurrection. It strikes me as strange that Christians are more concerned about the state of the nation than they are the state of the Church. Now let me say at once that every Christian ought to have a deep concern about the moral condition of our nation. We are at an all-time low spiritually and morally.

Every year we kill millions of babies in the womb, we treat the Ten Commandments as if they were a joke, we consider education to be the means of our salvation, we allow our airwaves to carry the most poisonous and pernicious images and the most foul language, marriage is being mocked, there is corruption in high places, our courts are slow to punish evildoers, teenage pregnancies are the highest in Europe, gambling is becoming a powerful addiction for many and things are happening that cry out to high heaven.

There is a great deal to feel concerned about as we focus on the state of the nation and the world but when it comes to the issue of revival, to focus primarily on the needs of the nation is beginning at the wrong end. Certainly there is room for criticism and concern out there, but the strongest criticism and concern must be reserved for ourselves. The initial focus should be on ourselves, what kind of people we are and what kind of people we should be.

Now there are many people who would regard themselves as people of God because they believe in a Creator. So God puts it beyond all doubt when He says:

'If my people WHO ARE CALLED BY MY NAME ...'

And who are those who are called by His name? Well, those who have first called upon His name. Scripture says that 'whoever calls on the name of the Lord shall be saved'. If you haven't called on the name of the Lord in a personal way, then gently I say it, you cannot claim to be one of His people. You can go to church, live a life that is well within the law, be religious, even take Holy Communion, but if you have not called on Him personally then you cannot claim to be one of His people.

You see, going to a church does not make you a Christian any more than going to the theatre makes you an actor. God chooses to begin with His own Church when He offers revival and that puts upon us an enormous responsibility. Not one person, but all His people. His true people that is.

'If my people who are called by my name, WILL HUMBLE THEMSELVES ...'

Now I find this statement very interesting. It is a popular belief amongst the majority of Christians that revival begins with prayer. But, according to this text, that is not so. Before we get down on our knees, God says there is something we have to do before we open our mouths in prayer. And what is that? We are to humble ourselves.

There are many fallacies in the Christian Church as to what it means to be humble. In a church of which I was once the pastor I remember giving an address on the subject of humility and afterwards a woman came up to me and said, 'I did so much enjoy your address. Humility is a favourite topic of mine. I believe it to be one of my greatest qualities.'

Humility is best understood perhaps when we look at the opposite of the word. And what is that? Pride. C.S. Lewis once said – and heed this carefully:

If you want to know how much pride you have ask yourself how much you dislike it in others. If you think you are not conceited then it means you are very conceited indeed for the first step to requiring humility is to realise that one is proud. We are all full of pride but we can't see it. It blinds us to our own condition. So it is wise to admit it even though you do not see it or feel it. There can be no surer proof of a confirmed pride than a belief that one is sufficiently humble.[1]

His point is that you don't have to *feel* humble, you just have to admit it. True humility is seen when we are willing to bring our lives under the authority of God's Word and evaluate ourselves not by the standards of society but by the standards of God. We best humble ourselves when we lay our lives alongside the Bible, to see it for what it is – God's authoritative Word – and be eager to obey its commands. We need the attitude that will not stand in judgment over it but sit under it in humility. To be quick and eager to respond to everything God asks of us in His Word. Not slowly or grudgingly but giving God the benefit of every doubt. To the best of my knowledge there has never been a spiritual revival amongst people who did not believe or accept the Bible.

I have no hesitation in saying that pride is the biggest impediment to revival. It is an implacable enemy of God. God resists the proud, says Scripture. And 'there can be no surer proof of a confirmed pride than a belief that one is sufficiently humble'.

'If my people who are called by my name, will humble themselves
AND PRAY ...'
Ah now you may be feeling somewhat relieved as we move away from the subject of pride and you may say to yourself: Well I may have some

pride in me but this is a test I can pass – I do pray. Do you? How much? How sincerely?

When did you last stay up late just to pray? We pray with the rest of the people in a group but how much time do we spend before God privately in prayer?

Revival praying is focused praying, unhurried praying, waiting on God and pleading with Him to open the heavens. It is not prayers that have a breathless eagerness about them to get them finished. It is passionate praying, persistent praying, intensive praying. We long for revival but we are not willing to pay the price. Someone put it like this: 'Please excuse me from the Upper Room but call me when the fire falls.' We will probably not see revival until we can't live without it. And the only word I can think of to sum up that is 'desperate'. Revival praying is desperate praying.

Prayer opens us up to God's great power. All around us the power of God is present and it breaks through to us at the point of prayer. Billy Graham says God's power is like an inverted triangle. A little prayer and a little power comes in. A lot and a lot flows. All around us the power of God is flowing and it comes in at the place of prayer.

That's the kind of praying God is thinking about when He lays down the conditions for revival. And that costs something. It suggests a passion that says, 'O God, we cannot live without revival ... we cannot go on like this ... Oh God, please, please send revival. We can't live like this.' Revival praying is when we are filled with a holy desperation. When we humble ourselves and pray like this, with passion, with fervour, with a sense of holy desperation, we will be getting close to revival.

God qualifies the issue by saying this:

'If my people who are called by my name, will humble themselves and pray AND SEEK MY FACE ...'

What does that mean? Far too often we are more interested in seeing the hand of God at work than we are in seeing His face. We want to see the sick healed, we want to see supernatural events taking place (there is nothing wrong with that), but revival praying puts as its priority to have a new vision of God, a new understanding of Him, a new and deeper relationship with Him, to know God for Himself not just for what He can give but for who He is.

Is there a prayer group for revival in your church? If not, then for heaven's sake start one. Or join one of the prayer groups in the area where people meet to pray for revival. Listen to what Isaiah said about this kind of praying: 'You who call on the LORD, give yourselves no rest, and give him no rest till he establishes Jerusalem and makes her the praise of the earth' (Isa. 62:6–7).

Our text continues:

'If my people who are called by my name, will humble themselves and pray and seek my face AND TURN FROM THEIR WICKED WAYS ...'

Wicked ways? The people of God with wicked ways? Surely not. It means silly ways perhaps, careless ways even but surely not wicked ways. Wicked is not a word we would want applied to us I imagine.

What are some of those wicked ways God is talking about? Well, let's start with the fact of our Christian disunity that shows to the world a fragmented picture of the Saviour. How snobbish and suspicious one church can be of another. It is breaking down in some places, of course, and there are many towns where churches and ministers are joining together to pray for revival. But there is still far too much suspicion between churches and pride in denominations.

I don't think God is against our denominations. I think He just ignores them. God may not want to take you out of your denomination but He does want to take the denomination out of you. It's not our denominations that are the problem but denominationalism. It is a wicked way. Some churches would rather die in separation than live in fellowship.

Then what about our casual attitude to the Bible, our lukewarmness and lack of spiritual passion, our unwillingness to stand up and be counted, our tendency to compromise, our departure from our first love, our insensitivity to truth, our worldly attitudes, our low view of marriage with some Christian couples living together without marriage? Maybe we didn't realise how wicked these things were. And all are practised by people who claim to know the Way. Shame on us.

It is a tremendous responsibility to belong to the people of God. Every one of us carries a responsibility for the honour of God's name. People judge the Church by the impression that we make upon them. If anyone lapses and fails, they don't see that that person is just one of millions of people. They judge everyone else by that person. They don't see us as one of hundreds of millions; they observe our ways and they say to themselves, if that is what Christianity is all about then I want nothing to do with it. I'm missing nothing. If on the other hand we live right then they are affected in a positive way and think of others like that also.

Now some of these things might not be seen as serious in worldly people. But God's own people ... claiming to have the life of Christ in them, claiming to be new creatures? If we are in Christ and Christ is in us then the world has a right to expect us to be different. The late Cardinal Basil Hulme said, 'Christians should have about them "signs of contradiction".'

Now what does it mean to turn from our wicked ways? God uses another phrase for this in Scripture which is familiar to most of us but often it is not clearly understood. The New Testament concept for what God is saying here is this: repentance. Repentance is one of the most misunderstood words in the Christian vocabulary. People think repentance is feeling sorry for your sins. But that is not what the word is about.

The Greek word for repentance is metanoia which means a change of mind. It is good when we feel sorry for our 'wicked ways' but that is the outcome of repentance not the beginning of it. Repentance is seeing that the direction in which you are going is wrong then turning in a new direction with your thoughts, changing your mind, for example, about where your life is found.

The biggest mistake people make about repentance is that they expect to feel sorry about their sin before they repent. Repentance begins not by waiting to feel sorry about your sin but deciding in the light of God's Word how wrong it is and making up your mind to turn to God. It begins with a change of mind and when your mind is changed then … then your feelings feel the impact of that for our feelings follow our thoughts in the same way that ducks follow their mother on a pond.

So don't think because you don't have any deep feelings of sorrow or guilt that you are not required to repent. Don't wait for your feelings to be stirred. Think about it and change. Consider your ways, said the prophet Malachi to the people of his day. What we think about affects the way we feel. You take the first step and feelings will follow. Don't worry about the feelings. Do what is right and the rest will follow on as night follows day.

But what if we do what God asks? Listen! Listen!

'If my people who are called by my name, will humble themselves and pray and seek my face and turn from their wicked ways, THEN WILL I HEAR FROM HEAVEN ...'

Revival is heaven-sent. It doesn't come up from our clever ideas and conferences. It comes down from heaven. You can't light the fire on earth; it must come down from heaven. That is the only source. There is the promise. It is a promise of God. You can bank on it.

'If my people who are called by my name, will humble themselves and pray and seek my face and turn from their wicked ways, then will I hear from heaven AND WILL FORGIVE THEIR SIN ...'

Forgiveness, said someone, is the greatest hunger of the soul. This is what God offers us when we make up our minds to do what He asks. It floods our beings, releases us, and sets us on fire.

'If my people who are called by my name, will humble themselves and pray and seek my face and turn from their wicked ways, then will I hear from heaven and will forgive their sin AND WILL HEAL THEIR LAND'

True revival spills over into the non-Christian community and we can expect that when the Church is revived the nation will feel its effects. It is probably true to say that the spiritual state of the nation depends not so much what happens in the Houses of Parliament but what happens in the House of God.

In Wales in 1904 the whole nation was affected. Crime figures dropped, the economy was better, educational levels improved, there was less consumption of alcohol, and businesses ran better because people were more industrious.

Revival would

drastically reduce sleaze

pay off old debts

save the demise of the family

put moral fibre back into the nation

aid our economy

clean up our language

reduce sexual immorality

disinfect the media

lessen the prison population

improve the quality of our work

save our cities from ruin

restore to the nation a sense of destiny.

Well there it is. What are you now going to do about it? It is a lot to believe when we see our nation slipping into apostasy, when Christianity is declining, when sin is rampant and rife, when young people have no clear ethical guidelines, when postmodernism rules in our colleges and universities, when moral absolutes no longer prevail, when there is an undermining of so many things. But not to believe it would make God a liar. We must rest our whole weight upon it.

So hear again the merciful promise of an offended but compassionate God:

If my people, who are called by my name, will humble themselves and pray and seek my face and turn from their wicked ways, then will I hear from heaven and will forgive their sin and will heal their land.

NOTE

1. C.S. Lewis, *Mere Christianity* (Fount, 1997).

National Distributors

UK: (and countries not listed below)
CWR, Waverley Abbey House, Waverley Lane, Farnham, Surrey GU9 8EP.
Tel: (01252) 784700 Outside UK +44 1252 784700

AUSTRALIA: CMC Australasia, PO Box 519, Belmont, Victoria 3216.
Tel: (03) 5241 3288

CANADA: Cook Communications Ministries, PO Box 98, 55 Woodslee Avenue, Paris, Ontario.
Tel: 1800 263 2664

GHANA: Challenge Enterprises of Ghana, PO Box 5723, Accra.
Tel: (021) 222437/223249 Fax: (021) 226227

HONG KONG: Cross Communications Ltd, 1/F, 562A Nathan Road, Kowloon.
Tel: 2780 1188 Fax: 2770 6229

INDIA: Crystal Communications, 10-3-18/4/1, East Marredpalli, Secunderabad – 500026,
Andhra Pradesh.
Tel/Fax: (040) 27737145

KENYA: Keswick Books and Gifts Ltd, PO Box 10242, Nairobi.
Tel: (02) 331692/226047 Fax: (02) 728557

MALAYSIA: Salvation Book Centre (M) Sdn Bhd, 23 Jalan SS 2/64, 47300 Petaling Jaya, Selangor.
Tel: (03) 78766411/78766797 Fax: (03) 78757066/78756360

NEW ZEALAND: CMC Australasia, PO Box 36015, Lower Hutt.
Tel: 0800 449 408 Fax: 0800 449 049

NIGERIA: FBFM, Helen Baugh House, 96 St Finbarr's College Road, Akoka, Lagos.
Tel: (01) 7747429/4700218/825775/827264

PHILIPPINES: OMF Literature Inc, 776 Boni Avenue, Mandaluyong City.
Tel: (02) 531 2183 Fax: (02) 531 1960

SINGAPORE: Armour Publishing Pte Ltd, Block 203A Henderson Road,
11–06 Henderson Industrial Park, Singapore 159546.
Tel: 6 276 9976 Fax: 6 276 7564

SOUTH AFRICA: Struik Christian Books, 80 MacKenzie Street, PO Box 1144, Cape Town 8000.
Tel: (021) 462 4360 Fax: (021) 461 3612

SRI LANKA: Christombu Books, 27 Hospital Street, Colombo 1.
Tel: (01) 433142/328909

TANZANIA: CLC Christian Book Centre, PO Box 1384, Mkwepu Street, Dar es Salaam.
Tel/Fax: (022) 2119439

USA: Cook Communications Ministries, PO Box 98, 55 Woodslee Avenue, Paris, Ontario, Canada.
Tel: 1800 263 2664

ZIMBABWE: Word of Life Books (Pvt) Ltd, Christian Media Centre, 8 Aberdeen Road, Avondale,
PO Box A480 Avondale, Harare, Zimbabwe, Tel: (04) 333355 or 091301188

For email addresses, visit the CWR website: www.cwr.org.uk
CWR is a registered charity - Number 294387
CWR is a limited company registered in England - Registration Number
1990308.

My Story

Selwyn Hughes traces his story from his roots in Wales through his conversion and call to the ministry, to his experiences as a pastor and pioneer in the fields of Christian counselling and training

My Story tells how CWR has grown into an international Christian organisation respected for its excellence.

Selwyn bares his heart in telling of God's love, grace and strength upholding him through the loss of family members and in his battle with cancer.

The depth of Selwyn's love and relationship with God shines through making *My Story* both inspiring and faith building.

ISBN: 1-85345-296-3

£9.99 (plus p&p)

Every Day with Jesus

One of the most popular daily Bible study tools in the world with nearly a million readers per issue. This inspiring devotional is available bimonthly in regular or large print.

- Get practical help with life's challenges

- Gain insight into the deeper truths of Scripture

- Be challenged, comforted and encouraged

ISSN: 0967-1889

£1.99 (plus p&p) per issue

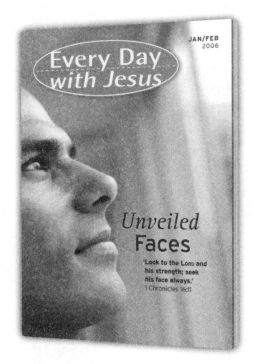

In September 2005, *Every Day with Jesus* celebrated its 40th anniversary. A special address from Selwyn Hughes was recorded at the anniversary celebration and is available on CD direct from CWR, price £3.99 (plus p&p).

To order, telephone 01252 784710 or shop online at www.cwrstore.org.uk

Prayer - A Fresh Vision

This book will encourage you to take a fresh look at your prayer life
and teach you how to offer effective prayers that touch the heart of
God and keep you in His will. Don't miss talking with your Father
in heaven and learning the essentials of effective prayer: worship and
adoration, thanksgiving and praise, petition and intercession, listening
and confession.

ISBN: 1-85345-308-0

£6.99 (plus p&p)

Revival - Times of Refreshing

Selwyn Hughes explores what revival really is – and isn't. He looks at past revivals to examine how we, and the Church as a whole, are prepared by God for revival so that we may know how to respond. Discover how to be the 'wire' along which God's power runs, bringing times of refreshing to His people.

ISBN: 1-85345-327-7

£6.99 (plus p&p)